T0149321

Carl Rogers
and
Paul Tillich
in
Dialogue:

A Mere Mortal Explores
an Interaction
Between Two Giants

Doug Bower

Carl Rogers and Paul Tillich in Dialogue:
A Mere Mortal Explores an Interaction Between Two Giants

iUniverse books may be ordered through booksellers or by contacting:

iUniverse
1663 Liberty Drive
Bloomington, IN 47403
www.iuniverse.com
1-800-Authors (1-800-288-4677)

Scripture quotations from the Holy Bible, King James Version (Authorized Version). First published in 1611. Quoted from the KJV Classic Reference Bible.

Scripture quotations marked NASB are taken from the New American Standard Bible®, Copyright © 1960, 1962, 1963, 1968, 1971, 1972, 1973, 1975, 1977, 1995 by The Lockman Foundation. Used by permission.

ISBN: 978-1-5320-8933-6 (sc)
ISBN: 978-1-5320-8934-3 (e)

Print information available on the last page.

iUniverse rev. date: 12/09/2019

Contents

Dedication

To my wife (Cheryl) and daughters (Katie & Erin) who probably would quickly understand how scrambled my dealing with Carl Rogers and Paul Tillich is. They would further understand how absurd it was/is to undertake this project. They would say, "Yep, that is what he would do, take on a project over his head."

Preface

About 1967, or 1968, during a class on Human Relations Training, the director of the nursing program, Georgene DeChow, gave a lecture/demonstration on Carl Rogers and his approach to relating to clients. Whether, she held Rogers and the client-centered approach up as the standard for relating I do not know. Myself, I was intimidated by the woman and in psychoanalytic jargon was transferring all sorts of perceptions on her in terms of power. At any rate during her demonstration she was using reflection as a model of relating. And during that demonstration one of my classmates started asking questions in regard to what he was witnessing. I recall he felt skeptical of the approach to relating to people in such a manner. In his interaction, as he expressed his skepticism, Ms. DeChow kept reflecting his comments and concerns. Suddenly, he sat down. He appeared to me to suddenly feel being had. His own points came back to him and he realized she simply was returning to him what he said. She didn't argue with him, she returned his own points to him. I don't know if he felt he was understood, but he certainly didn't feel he was dealing with someone who was telling him, at least overtly, that he was wrong.

I started moving in a direction of using reflection to engage people as a helper and sometimes as a friend as I have never really been much of a conversationalist and reflection helped keep me engaged. The presentation by Ms. DeChow was to my recollection was my first exposure to Rogers.

I know regard reflection as a superficial means of making empathic responses and seldom use it anymore, even as I profess the Person-Centered Approach as my basic model of counseling and relating. That breadth of that is beyond the scope of Preface.

Some years later while I was studying at Columbia Theological Seminary in Decatur, Georgia, I took a course under Ben Kline. Dr. Kline had a reputation in the seminary community as an expert on Paul Tillich. Indeed, the course was about Tillich. I remember getting my brain scrambled trying to grasp Tillich. I still get my brain scrambled trying to deal with Tillich. This project didn't fix that. Yet, I have found myself fascinated by Tillich whom I came to see as closet Lutheran. I have tried to speak to that in this work. I make no claim that I was successful as great Christian theologians share common perspectives and who is to say if any given adherent is a Luther, Calvinist, or Wesleyan based on the perspectives they espoused. Who is even to say for instance that Luther was a Lutheran or a whatever-an (Ok, I made that up for this Preface). No great thinker creates in a vacuum.

So, I hope in all this the reader while join in the puzzlement, the scrambledness, and then feel led to make his or her own attempts to develop a project dealing with these giants.

Carl Rogers - Paul Tillich Dialogue

(Part A)

In this verbatim, I tried to capture everything I could. It is not cleaned up to be grammatically correct. Thus, "ah" and "um" even show up. The speakers repeated their words. That too was captured. What you get is what I think I heard as best as I can convey it.

CARL ROGERS: The importance of self-affirmation: I think that would be one area where we agree. Then I have been much impressed with your thinking about the courage to be, because l that in psychotherapy; the courage of being something, the risk that is involved in knowing . . . . I've also liked your phrase about him the antimoral act being one that contradicts the realization of the individual, and it seems to me both of us are trying to push beyond some of the trends that are very prominent in the modern world; the logical positivistic, the ultra-scientific approach, the stress of the mechanistic and highly deterministic point of view which, as I see it, makes man just an object trying to find some alternative stance in relation to life. I wonder if you feel that we're in some agreement on issues of that sort.

PAUL TILLICH: Yes, of course. In all these points I heartily agree, and I am very glad you enumerate them for me.

ROGERS: Well, perhaps we could push into some areas where I am not quite so sure. I wonder what some of your views are about the nature of man. When I've been asked about that - I think some of the existentialists take the point of view that man really has no nature, but it seems to me that he has - I have taken the point of view that man belongs to a particular species. He has species characteristics. One of those, I think, being the fact that he has a . . . I think he is incurably social; I think he has a deep need for relationships. Then I think that simply because man is an organism, he tends to be directional. He's moving in the direction of actualizing himself. Ah . . . So, um . . . for myself, I really feel man does have a . . . a describable nature. I have been um interested, for example, in the fact that you discuss the demonic aspects of man. I don't know whether you see that as a part of his nature - at any rate I'd be . . . I'd be interested in your . . . in your views in regard to the nature of man.

TILLICH: Your question is very far-reaching and demands of me a little bit longer answer. Ah . . . The first point I want to make is that man, definitively, has a nature, and I think the best way to prove this is negatively, by showing how impossible it is if somebody denies that man has nature. I think of ah . . .the famous French existentialist, Sartre, who has denied that man has nature and has emphasized that man . . . man is everything he makes of himself and this is his freedom. But, if he says that this is man's freedom to make himself, then this, of course, means that he has a nature of freedom, which other species do not have. So, to make such statements is somehow self-contradictory. Even if you attribute to man what medieval theology attributed to God, namely, to be by himself, and not conditioned by anything else, even then you cannot escape the statement that man has a nature. Now that's my answer to the first element in your question, but there are two more and I want to get at them.

The ah . . . second is that I distinguish, so to speak, two natures of man, or one which one rightly calls his nature and the other which is a mixture of accepting and distorting his true nature. The first one I would call, with a very vague term, his true nature, but ah . . . to make it less vague I usually call it his essential nature. And if I speak theologically, then I call it man's created nature, and ah . . . you remember that this is one of the main points about which the early church was tremendously fighting – namely, that man's essential or created nature is good. According to the biblical word, "God looked at everything he had created and behold it was very good." And there is an even more philosophical, reformulated affirmation of this by Augustine, namely, *Esse qua esse bonum est*, which means in English, "being as being is good." Now that is what I would call man's essential nature. And then, from this, we must distinguish man's existential nature, of which I would say it has a characteristic of being estranged from his true nature. Man, as he is in time and space, in biography and history. And this man is not simply the opposite of man's essential nature, then it wouldn't be man any longer, but it is a distortion of this. And an attempt to reach it, are contradictory to reach his true nature, are contradicting his true nature. It is a tremendous mixture. And in order to understand the real human predicament, we must distinguish these two elements. I believe that in Freud, himself, and much Freudianism and generally psychotherapy, there is no clear distinction of these two points. This . . . this was your second element. Now shall I answer also your third element . . . ?

ROGERS: Let me . . . let me make one comment on this. I find in my work as a therapist that if I can create a um . . . a climate of the utmost of freedom for the other individual, that um . . . I can really trust the directions that he will move. That is, people sometimes say l to me "What if you create a climate of freedom? A man might ah . . . use that freedom to become completely evil or antisocial." I don't find that to be true, and and this is one of the things that makes me feel that um . . . I don't know whether this is essentially or existentially but ah . . . that in a in a relationship of of real freedom the individual tends to move toward ah . . . not only deeper self-understanding, but toward more social behavior.

TILLICH: Yes, now I would put a question mark to this, and I ah . . . would say that first of all, who is free enough to create this situation of freedom for the other? And since I call this mixture of ah . . . man's essential nature and his estranged nature ambiguous – the realm of the ambiguity of life – I would say under the condition of this ambiguity, nobody is able to create this sphere of freedom. But now let's suppose that it exists in some other way. I can come to this later when we speak of the demonic. Then I still would say the individual who lives in such a social group in which freedom is given to him remains an ambiguous mixture between essential and existential being. He is, as the English language expresses it beautifully, in a predicament, and this predicament is universal tragic estrangement from one's true being. Therefore, I don't believe in the power of the individual to use his freedom in the way in which he should, namely, fulfilling one's own essential potentialities, or essentialities; these two words are here the same. So, I am ah . . . more skeptical, both about the creation of such a situation and about the individuals who are in such a situation.

ROGERS: I would agree on the difficulty of ah . . . creating ah . . . complete freedom. I am sure none of us is ever able to really create that for another person in its completeness. Yet what impresses me is that even imperfect attempts to ah . . . um . . . create a climate of freedom and and acceptance and understanding ah . . . seem to liberate the person to move toward um . . . toward really social goals. I wonder if it is your um thinking about the ah . . . demonic aspect that that makes you put a question mark after that.

TILLICH: Now, let me first answer you about what you just said, and here I would very much agree. I would say there are ah . . . fragmentary actualizations in history and I agree especially with the ah . . . deep insight we have gained, largely by psychotherapy, about the tremendous importance of love in earliest ages of the development of child . . . children. So, the question would come here: "Where are the forces which create a situation in which the child receives that love which gives him, later on, the freedom to face life and not to escape from life into neuroses and psychoses?" And I leave that question open.

But ah . . . now you are interested about the demonic, and you are not the only one. I myself was, and everybody is in some way, so let me say how I came to this concept. I wrote in the year 1926, when I was still professor in the University of ah . . . Dresden Germany, a little article, a little pamphlet, *The Demonic*, and the reason not to speak of the fallen men or the sinful men or any of these phrases was that I saw from two points of view structures which are stronger than the good will of the individual, and one of these structures was the neurotic-psychotic structure. I came into contact after the First World War, since 1920 about, with the psychoanalytic movement, coming from Freud at that time, and changing the climate ah . . . of the whole century already in Europe at the time. The second was the analysis of the conflicts of society by the Socialist movement and especially by the early writings of Karl Marx, and in both cases, I found a phenomenon for which these traditional terms, like "fallen men" and "sinful men," are not sufficient. The only sufficient term I found in the New Testament use was the term "demonic," which is in the stories about Jesus, similar to being possessed. That means being in a force, ah . . . under a force, which is stronger than the individual good will. And so, I used that term. Of course, I emphasized very much, I don't mean it in a mythological sense, as little demons or a personal Satan running around the world, but I mean it as structures which are ambiguous, both to a certain extent creative, but ultimately destructive. And ah . . . this is the reason why I introduced that term. So, instead of only speaking of estranged mankind, and not using the old terminology anyhow, I had to find a term which covers the transpersonal power which takes hold of men and of society; ah . . . of men in stages, let's say, of drunkenness, being a drunkard, and not being able to overcome it, or ah . . .

producing a society in which either class conflicts or as today in the whole world, conflicts of great ideologies, of great forms of political faiths which struggle with each other, and every step to overcome them has usually the consequence of driving the people more deeply into them. Now this is what I meant with the demonic. So, I hope I made one thing clear: that I don't mean it in the old mythological sense which of course has to be demythologized.

ROGERS: . . . And certainly, ah um . . . when I look at some of the things going on in the world from the power point of view and so on, I can see why you might think in terms of ah . . . demonic structures.

I'd like to talk a little bit about the way I see the um . . . ah . . . this matter of ah . . . alienation and estrangement. It seems to me that the . . . the infant is not estranged from himself. To me it seems that the infant is a . . . is a whole and integrated ah . . . organism, gradually individual, and that the estrangement that occurs is one that he learns, that . . . that in order to um . . . preserve the love of others, parents usually, he takes into himself as something he has experienced for himself, the judgments of his parents: just like the ah . . . small boy who has been rebuked for pulling his sister's hair goes around saying, "bad boy, bad boy." Meanwhile, he is pulling her hair again. In other words, he has introjected the notion that he is bad, where actually he is enjoying the experience, and it is this estrangement between what he is experiencing and the concepts he links up with what he is experiencing that seems to me to constitute the ah . . . the basic ah . . . estrangement. Um . . . I don't know whether you want to comment on that because I also want to get into the kind of thing that ah . . . heals up the relationship, but perhaps you . . .

TILLICH: Yes, ah . . . because ah . . . the infant is a very important problem. I call in ah . . . more philosophical or, better, psychological terms, the mythological state of Adam and Eve before the Fall: dreaming innocence. It has not yet reached reality. It is still dreaming. Of course, this also is a symbol, but it is a symbol which is nearer to our psychological language than the ah . . . ah . . . Fall of Adam and Eve. ah . . . But it means the same thing, and it means that Adam, namely men - the Hebrew "Adam" means men – that men, every man, is in the process of transition from dreaming innocence to conscious self-actualization, and in this process the estrangement also takes place, as well as the fulfillment; therefore, my concept of ambiguity. And ah . . . I agree with you ah . . . that there is also in what the parents used to call ah . . . "bad boy" or "bad girl," there is also a necessary act of self-fulfillment, but there is also something asocial in it, because it hurts his sister and so it has to be repressed, and whether we say "bad boy," or prevent it in any other way, this is equally necessary, and these experiences ah . . . mean for me the slow process of transition from dreaming innocence into self-actualization on the one side and self-estrangement on the other side, and these two acts are ambiguously intermixed. Now that would be about my interpretation of ah . . . the ah . . . situation of the infants.

ROGERS: Well, there is much in that that ah . . . I would agree with. I'd like to say a little bit about the ah . . . kind of relationship in which I think ah . . . man's estrangement can be healed, as I see it from my own experience. For example, when we talk about – when either of us talk about the courage to be or the tendency to become one-self, I feel that perhaps that can only be fully achieved in a . . . in a relationship. Ah . . . Perhaps the . . . the best example of what I am talking about is that um . . . I believe that the person can only accept the unacceptable in himself when he is in a close relationship in which he experiences acceptance. This . . . this, I think, is a large share of what ah . . . ah . . . what constitutes psychotherapy, that the individual finds that the feelings he has been ah . . . ashamed of or that he has been unable to admit ah . . . into his awareness ah . . ., that those can be accepted by another person, so then he becomes able to accept them as a part of himself. Ah . . . I don't know too much of your thinking about ah . . . interpersonal relationships, but I wonder how that ah . . . how that ah . . . how that sounds to you.

TILLICH: I believe that you are absolutely right in saying that without the man-to-man experience of forgiveness, or better, acceptance of the unacceptable, is a very necessary ah . . . precondition for self-affirmation. And you cannot forgive yourself, you cannot accept yourself. If you look in the spiritual mirror, then you are much more prone to hate yourself and to be disgusted with yourself. So I believe that all the ah . . . forms of confessional in the churches and the confessions between friends and married people, and now the psychoanalytic ah . . . confession of one's deeper levels which are opened up by the analyst – that without these things, there is no possibility of experiencing something of which however, I would say, it belongs ultimately in a . . . to another dimension: the dimension of the ultimate, let me call it preliminarily. But ah . . . I would say, with you, only the right acceptance is the medium through which it is necessary ah . . . men have to go - from men to men - before the dimension of the ultimate is possible. And ah . . . I may add here that I have not used often anymore the word "forgiveness," because this often produces a bad superiority in him who forgives and the humiliation of him who is forgiven. Therefore, I prefer the concept of acceptance. And ah . . . if ah . . . you accept this acceptance, then I think I can confess that I have learned it from psychoanalysis. I have learned to translate an ideological concept which doesn't communicate any longer ah . . . and replaced it by the way in which the psychoanalyst accepts his patients: not judging him, not telling him you must first he should be good, otherwise I cannot accept you, but accepting him just because he is not good, but he has something in himself which wants to be good.

ROGERS: Certainly, in my own experience, the ah . . . the potency of acceptance of another person has been demonstrated time and time again, when an individual feels that he is ah . . . both fully accepted in all that he has been able to express and yet prized as a person. This has a very potent influence on his ah . . . life and on his behavior.

TILLICH: Yes, now I believe that this is really the center of what we call the "good news" in the Christian message, which . . .

Carl Rogers - Paul Tillich Dialogue

(Part B)

[Intermission.]

TILLICH: The minister, who represents the ultimate meaning of life, can have much skill unconsciously, although he is unskilled, but even then he should not establish himself as a ah . . . second . . . second-rate psychotherapist. Now that seems to me ah . . . a very important rule. Otherwise, ah . . . cooperation would soon end in little catastrophes and would come to an end altogether.

ROGERS: Well, that sort of sets off in me a somewhat um . . . deeper question. I realize very well that I and many other therapists are interested in the kind of issues that ah . . . involve the ah . . . religious worker and the theologian, and yet um . . ., for myself, I prefer to put my thinking on those issues in humanistic terms, or or to attack those issues through through the channels of ah . . . of scientific investigation. I guess I have some real um . . . sympathy for the modern view that is sort of symbolized in the phrase that "God is"; that is, that religion no longer does speak to people in the modern world, and um . . . I I would be interested in knowing why you tend to put your thinking – which certainly is very congenial to that of ah . . . a number of psychologists these days – why you tend to put your thinking in religious ah . . . terminology and theological ah . . . language.

TILLICH: Now, I think that is a very large question . . .

ROGERS: Yes, it sure is . . .

TILLICH: . . . and it could take all our time, so I want to confine myself to a few points. Now, first, the fundamental point is that I believe, metaphorically speaking, man lives not only in the horizontal dimension, namely the relationship of himself as a finite being to other finite beings, observing them and managing them, but he also has in himself something which I call, metaphorically, the vertical line; the line not to a heaven with God and other beings in it, but what I mean with the vertical line is towards something which is not transitory and finitude and finite; something which is infinite, unconditional, ultimate – I usually call it. Man has an experience in himself that he is more than a piece of finite objects which come and go. He experiences something beyond time and space. I don't speak here – I must emphasize this in speeches again and again – in terms of life after death, or in other symbols which cannot be used in this way anymore, but I speak of the immediate experience of the temporal, of the eternal in the temporal, or of the temporal invaded by the eternal in some moments of our life and of the life together with other people and of the group life. Now, that is for me the reason why I try to continue to interpret the great traditional religious symbols as relevant for us: because I know, and that was the other point you made, that they have become largely irrelevant, and that we cannot use them in the way in which they are used still very much in preaching, and religious teaching, and liturgies, for people who can live in them, who are not by critical analysis estranged from them, but for those large amounts of people whom you call humanists, we need a translation and interpretation of these symbols, but not, as you seem to indicate, a replacement. I don't believe that scientific language is able to express the vertical dimension adequately, because it is bound to the relationship of finite things to each other, even in psychology and certainly in all physical sciences. This is the reason why I think we need another language, and this language is the language of symbols and myths; it is a religious language. But we poor theologians, in contrast to you happy psychologists, are in the bad situation that we know the symbols with which we deal have to be reinterpreted and even radically reinterpreted. But ah . . . I have taken this heavy yoke upon myself and I have decided long ago I will continue to the end with it.

ROGERS: Well, I realized ah . . . as you were talking, I have a sort of a fantasy of this ah . . . vertical dimension not, for me not go . . ., not going up, but going down. Ah . . . What I mean is this: I um . . . I feel at times when I'm when I'm really being helpful to a client of mine, in those ah . . . sort of rare moments when there is something approximating an I-Thou relationship between us, and when ah . . . I feel that something significant is happening, then ah . . . I feel as though I am somehow in tune with the forces in the universe or that ah . . . ah . . . forces are operating through me in in in regard to this helping relationship that um . . . Well, I guess I feel somewhat the way the scientist does when he um . . . ah . . . is able to bring about ah . . . the ah . . . splitting of the atom. He didn't ah . . . crack it with his own little hands, but he ah . . . nevertheless put himself in line with the significant forces of the universe and thereby was able to ah . . . ah . . . trigger off a significant event, and I feel much the same way, I think, ah . . . ah . . . Trigger off a significant event, and I feel much the same way, I think, ah . . . ah . . . oftentimes, in dealing with a client when I really am being helpful.

TILLICH: I am very grateful about what you say. Now, the first words were especially interesting to me, when you said a vertical line has always an up and a down. And ah . . . you will be interested to hear from me that I am accused very often by my theological colleagues that I speak much too much of down, instead of up, and that's true; when I want to give a name for what I am about ultimately concerned, then I call it the "ground of being" and ground is, of course, down and not up - so I go with you down. Now the question is, ah . . . where to do we go? And ah . . . here again I had the feeling I could go ah . . . far away ah . . . with you when you use the term "universe," forces of the universe, but ah . . . when I speak of "ground of being," I don't understand this depth of the universe in terms of an addition of all elements in the universe, of all single things, but, as many philosophers and theologians did, the creative ground of the universe, that out of which all these forms and elements come: and ah . . . I call it the creative ground. And this was the second point in which I was glad. This creative ground can be experienced in everything which is rooted in the creative ground. For instance, in a person-to-person encounter – and I had without being an analyst, but in many forms of encounters with human beings, very similar experiences as you, and now there is something present which transcends the limited reality of the Thou and the Ego of the other one and of myself, and ah . . . I sometimes called it at special moments the presence of the holy, in a nonreligious conversation. That I can experience and have experienced, and I agree with you.

And then finally, there was your third point about the scientists, and I often told my scientist friends that ah . . . they follow strictly the principle formulated classically by Thomas Aquinas, the great medieval theologian: If you know something, then you know something about God. And ah . . . I would agree with this statement and ah . . . therefore these men also have an experience of what I like to call the ah . . . vertical line, down and perhaps also up, although what they do in splitting atoms is discovering and managing finite relations to each other.

ROGERS: I'd like to um . . . shift to another topic that has been of interest to me and I suspect may be of interest to you. Ah . . . this is the question of what constitutes the optimal person. In other words, ah . . . what is it that we're working toward, whether in therapy or ah . . . in the area of religion? For myself, I have a um . . . um . . . rather simple ah . . . definition, yet one which I think has a good many implications. I feel that ah . . . I'm quite pleased in my work as a therapist if I find that ah . . . my client and I, too, are ah . . . if we are both moving toward what I think of as greater openness to experience. If if the individual is becoming more able to listen to what's going on within himself, more sensitive to the reactions he's having to a given situation, if he's more accurately perceptive of the ah . . . world around him, both the world of reality and the world of relationships, ah . . . then I think ah . . . my feeling is I will be pleased. That's that's the direction I would hope we would move, because then he will be in the process, first of all, he will be in process all the time. He won't . . . this isn't a static kind of a goal for an individual. And um . . . he will be in the ah . . . process of becoming more fully himself. He'll also be um . . . ah . . . realistic, in the best sense, in that he's realistic about what is going on within himself, as well as realistic about the world, it's um . . . and I think he will also be in the process of becoming more ah . . . social simply because ah . . . one of the elements which he can't help but actualize in himself is the ah . . . ah . . . need and desire for closer human relationships. So, ah . . . for me, this ah . . . concept of ah . . . openness to experience describes a good deal of what I would ah . . . hope to see in the ah . . . more optimal person, whether we're talking about the person who emerges from therapy, or the development of a good citizen, or whatever. I wonder if you would have any comments on that or on your own point of view in that area.

TILLICH: Yes, there are two questions in this. The one is the way, namely the openness, and the other is the aim. It is, of course, not a static aim, not a dynamic aim, but it's an aim. And ah . . . let me speak to both points. Ah . . . the openness is a word ah . . . which is very familiar to myself because there are many questions a theologian is asked, and which can be answered only by the concept of openness, or opening up. Ah . . . I will give you two examples. The one example is the function of classical symbols and symbols generally. I always used to answer: Symbols open up, they open up reality and they open up something in us. If this word were not forbidden in the university today, I would call it something in our soul, but you know, as myself, as a psychologist, as somebody who deals with the soul, that the word "soul" is forbidden in academic contexts. But that's what symbols do, and they do it not only to individuals, they do it also to groups and usually only through groups to individuals. So that's the one thing where I use the word "open." This seems to me one of the main functions, perhaps the main function of symbols, namely, to open up. Then another use of the word "open" is that I am asked, now what can I do to experience God or to get the Divine Spirit or things like that? My answer is, the only thing you can do is keep yourselves open. You cannot force God down. You cannot ah . . . produce the Divine Spirit in yourselves, but what you can do is open yourself, to keep yourself open for it. And ah . . . this is, of course, in your terminology, a particular experiences experience, but we must keep open for all experiences. So, I would agree very much with the way that you have described. I would even believe that in all experiences, there is a possibility of having an ultimate experience.

Then, the aim: now, the aim ah . . . is ah . . . the many folds we discussed. Perhaps we could agree about realization of our true self, bringing into actuality what is essentially given to us; or, when I speak in religious symbolism, I could say: to become the way in which God sees us, in all our potentialities. And what that now practically is, is the next and very important question. You also indicated something of this: namely, to become social. I think this is a part of a larger concept. I would call it love, in the sense of the Greek word agape, which is a particular word in the New Testament, and which means that love which is described by Paul in I Corinthians 13, and which accepts the other as a person and then tries to reunite with him and to overcome the separation, the existential separation, which exists between men and men. Now, this aim, I would agree; but I would add, of course, since I speak also in terms of the vertical dimension, that ah . . . it is the keeping to that dimension to ah . . . maintain in the faith into an ultimate meaning of life, and the absolute and unconditional seriousness of this direction of this ultimate aim of life. So when I shall speak now in popular terms, it's very dangerous always, I would say: faith and love are the two concepts which are necessary, but faith not in the sense of beliefs but in the sense of being related to the ultimate, and love not in sense of any sentimentality, but in a sense of affirming the other person and even one's own person, because I believe with Augustine, and Erich Fromm, and others, that there is a justified self-affirmation and self-acceptance. I wouldn't use the term "self-love" – that's too difficult – but self-affirmation and self-acceptance, one of the most difficult things to reach.

ROGERS: No, I I find that I um . . . like it best when you become concrete; that is, when you put like . . . it in terms of faith and love. Those are . . . those can be very abstract ah . . . concepts which ah . . . can have all kinds of ah . . . different meanings, but the ah . . . ah . . . putting it in the concrete: yes, I do feel that the person does have to gain a ah . . . I wouldn't even hesitate to say, he has to gain a real appreciation of or liking of himself, ah . . . ah if he is going to affirm himself in a ah . . . healthy and and useful fashion. There's one other corollary to this um . . . notion of um . . . being open to experience that ah . . . we might explore a bit, too. I . . . to me, the individual who is reasonably open to his experience um . . . is involved in a continuous valuing process. That is, I think that um . . . I I realize that I've sort of dropped the notion of values in the conventional sense of there being certain values which you could list, and that kind of thing, but it does seem to me that the individual who is open to his experience is continually valuing each moment and valuing his behavior in each moment, as to whether it is ah . . . ah . . . related to his own self-fulfillment, his own actualization, and that um . . . it's that kind of ah . . . valuing process that to me ah . . . makes sense in the mature person. Ah . . . it also makes sense in a world where um . . . the whole situation is changing so rapidly that I I feel that ah . . . ordinary lists of values ah . . . are probably not as ah . . . appropriate or meaningful as they were ah . . . in periods gone by.

TILLICH: Yes. Now I am an outspoken critic of the philosophy of values, so I certainly agree with you. I replace ah . . . this thing by my concept of agape, or love - namely, love which is listening. I call it listening love, which doesn't follow abstract valuations, but which is ah . . . related to the concrete situation. And out of its listening to this very moment gains its decision for action and its inner feeling of satisfaction and even joy or dissatisfaction and bad conscience.

ROGERS: I like that phrase because I think it could be a listening within, a listening to oneself, as well as a listening love for the other ah . . . individual.

TILLICH: Yes, when I say listening to the situation, I mean the situation is ah . . . constituted out of everything around me and myself; so, listening love is always listening to both sides.

ROGERS: Well, that certainly ah . . . I I feel we're not very far apart in our thinking about this ah . . . value approach; I thought we might be further apart than we ah . . . seem to be. But, ah . . . one other instance: I feel that ah . . . the small infant is a good example of a valuing process that is going on continuously. He's ah . . . ah . . . he isn't troubled by the concepts and standards that have been built up for adults, and he's continually valuing his experience as being either making for his enhancement or ah . . . being ah . . . opposed to that ah . . . actualization.

TILLICH: Now, this valuation, of course, would be not an intellectual valuation, but an evaluation with his whole being . . .

ROGERS: I think of it as an organismic valuing process.

TILLICH: That means a reaction of his whole being, and I certainly believe that it is an adequate description and can help very much to come to a better . . . (The recording ends here with an announcer speaking over the closing comments). (Robert Lee, Producer, and Thomas D. Skinner, Director, Western Behavioral Sciences Institutes, La Jola, CA, Radio Television, San Diego State)

Opening Comments

This is critical, but friendly material. That means I disagree and prize what I saw. I approached the project as a conservative Christian. I dislike that label as it conjures up negativity in some circles. I also dislike the label "Rogerian" as it conjures up limits that are restrictive. I do have some room for calling myself an existentialist though my brand of existentialism influenced by the work of Ecclesiastes in the Old Testament. I have room for gloom, doom, despair and anxiety. The optimistic view of Carl Rogers counters that. I have however been influenced by Carl Rogers and engaged Tillich's material many times. The person-centered approach introduced to counseling, psychotherapy, and psychology by Rogers is the model I use.

On Rogers

While studying nursing at Manatee Jr. College in Bradenton, FL in the late 60s, I received a superficial exposure to Carl Rogers. I was taking a required course on Interpersonal Relationship Training.

During one of the classes, the director of the nursing program made a brief presentation. As she offered points on her take on the Rogerian approach to IPR, one of the students began asking questions about the approach. He sounded rather skeptical to me. The student became frustrated during the interaction. The intensity of his responses grew and escalated. He sounded angry to me.

The professor kept repeating parts of what the student said. It was that old unfortunate model of virtually parroting what the other person was saying.

Student: "I have doubts this approach is any good."

Professor: "You have doubts that the approach is any good."

This went on for several minutes. Suddenly, the student's demeanor changed. I do not remember if I thought he thought he had been had, or if he had an ah-ha experience. I tend to think that I felt he believed he had been had. There was no way to get to his point, which I thought was to feel connected and heard. He suddenly sat down and said no more.

My perception of the approach though from that point on was about repeating back to the client what the person said. I practiced that stereotypical response a variety of times of the years.

It was not until the early 80s that this changed. I took a course at the University of Georgia on theories of counseling and psychotherapy. Up until that time I held a narrow-minded view that the psychodynamic/psychoanalytic view was the only real kind of therapy. Yet, I never really could get fully immersed in the skill of interpretation and the methods involved with this area.

In some ways, it was rather fun to interpret the behaviors of others. However, I often found myself out of sync with the interpretations of peers regarding clients. I often was even more out of sync with the interpretations of supervisors in relationship to me. Sometimes they were right on target and even triggered cathartic experiences and personal revelations. Other times they were so off target that they felt invasive.

When I got a chance to line up various theories, primarily using Corey (1982), I found that my basic behavior was very congruent with the person-centered approach presented by Carl Rogers. Also,

I felt it was very helpful to study with a person who was committed to the approach rather than giving lip-service to the approach in lectures.

I began to embrace the approach. I felt my own reputation grew as I began to meet a host of contributors to the approach, Fred Zimring, Barbara Brodley, Bob Lee, John Shlien, Nat Raskin, John Woods, Chuck Stuart and others. Their names are readily found among the person-centered literature. In addition, I was developing a network of peers. I'd love to mention them, but I don't have their permission as we have gone our separate ways.

For several years, I believed I held a fundamental stance with the approach, though I harbored doubts about the basic goodness of human beings, unconditional positive regard, nonjudgmentalness, and nondirectiveness. I was also reluctant to call myself person-centered.

My doubts exploded in my own mind leading to reclaiming a position that, while human beings are good, there is an evil in human behavior that leads to war, crime, and oppression. I was not willing to attribute that "evil" to influences from society alone. It seemed to me that individuals were quite capable of doing awful things on their own. In addition, I saw some mean behaviors exhibit themselves among the person-centered community. I began to doubt that unconditional positive regard or nonjudgmentalness and became incredulous about its use. Later I began to view the insistence that real person-centered practitioners be nondirective as a form of directiveness. I replaced some of these concepts (Bower, 2011) and addressed them within the community, especially on the Internet ad nauseam.

I now see the approach radically differently than I did following my first exposure to it in the late 60s.

On Tillich

My exposure to Paul Tillich was far more flabbergasting. Tillich is far too left brain oriented for my right brain functioning. I had the opportunity to tackle some of Tillich's thinking at Columbia Theological Seminary in Decatur, GA as I studied with Ben Kline. Dr. Kline's reputation at the seminary was one of being an expert on Tillich.

I remember writing a paper for the course I took and expressing some dismay, that Tillich had a reputation as a womanizer. Being a rather self-righteous judgmental person at the time, I was aghast at this. I was quite hard on Tillich in that paper. I am sure in being so hard-nosed that, I missed a great deal of what Tillich had to say. Now, I cannot point to where I saw that tabloid type reputation and certainly cannot vouch for its accuracy. Indeed, I only discovered recently discovered information that indicated Tillich was not the womanizer that myths portrayed (May, 1973). You can see that information was around for over 40 years.

I am far from being an expert on Paul Tillich. I am still too right brain oriented to deal with his material. He is too abstract for me, but when I can cut through that abstractness, I rather like what I can grasp of the concepts of the courage to be; ground of being; and ultimate concern. I would not have the audacity myself to attempt to explain these concepts here. They represent a different intellectual paradigm than the one in which I function.

In the late 80's, early 90s, I discovered to Kirschenbaum & Henderson's (1989) work, Carl Rogers: Dialogues. It features interactions with Tillich, Skinner, Bateson, Polanyi, and May. While I have had the material in my personal library for nearly 20 years, I only read the interaction with Rollo May. My exploration of that led to the basic condition of humankind as being good and/or bad. I essentially reclaimed a position I had shelved that humankind is both.

However, in the last few months, that is late 2008 and early 2009, I began reexploring the quest for the historical Jesus material. I had viewed that quest through mythological glasses. I perceived it has dismissive rather than affirming of faith. It is my experience there is truth in my perception. However, Schweitzer (2005) whom I had seen as a ringleader in this skepticism was not as friendly to the quest as I thought. I also discovered the writing of Martin Kahler (1964). Writing in the late 1890s, I found he was raising issues and questions concerning the quest for the historical Jesus that were similar to my own.

Paul Tillich wrote the Forward to the (1964) translation of Kahler's work. In that work, Rudolf Bultmann's name came up. Bultmann was in the thick of the historical critical approach to exploring Scripture.

I read Bultmann several times and struggled with his concept of demythologization. Though I feel inadequate to attempt to define what Bultmann meant by that term, I believe it to speak to that offered by both Tillich and Rogers. I make no claim they deliberately intended to comply with Bultmann's dream of articulating faith in contemporary times.

I am presenting these names because they all had to be dealt with regarding the historical Jesus, and the historical-critical methodologies. In dealing with them, the name of Paul Tillich kept appearing. The point of which is to affirm that Tillich was a major player and contributor to what was going in the last century.

On Rogers and Tillich

So, in this circular pilgrimage is a rationalization of dealing with the Rogers-Tillich dialogue. In part, I assert they were offering perspectives, one secular through the filters of one raised in a Christian Reformed tradition, and one theological from one through the filters of one raised in a Lutheran tradition who remained in the domain of the sacred, sacred in the sense of it connection to Christian faith.

Several years ago, I attempted to get an audio copy of the dialogue for a colleague in Greece. However, the copy was of such poor quality that I could not justify sending it.

I later found that a film version is available on the Internet on YouTube. At this writing part 1 and part 2 of the Rogers - Tillich dialogue is available for viewing at http://www.carlrogers.info/video. html. However, as quickly as Websites change, this source is no longer accessible. The material was associated with the Archives, at the University of Santa Barbara, California.

This is the easy part, sharing my pilgrimage. The hard part follows for to go there I will be moving into left-brain activity with which I do not feel comfortable.

The Lost Introduction

In comparing the tape recording, I mentioned just above I found out that the poor quality seemed related to the recording at the wrong speed. Having obtained a cassette recorder for recording at slower speeds, I transferred the material from the micro cassette to a traditional cassette. Then I sped up the recorder to play the sound at what would have been a normal flow of conversation. This only verified the poor quality of the material. However, there were a few minutes of uncaptured monologue on the tape, which is apparently, is not available in transcript form. The tape is of such poor quality that there is no information as to its source. It would be great to offer specific information for citation. However, that information is missing. The introduction is missing in several sources of the

Tillich/Rogers interaction: (Kirschsenbaum & Henderson, 1989); (Rogers & Tillich, 2006); (Cooper, 2006).

The best I can do is capture the following from Rogers on the noisy garbled tape.

[Garbled] "The world renowned philosophical theologian at a conference arranged by members of our staff here at San Diego in March 1965. I was out of town when the conference started but returned in time to hear some of his talks. When I arrived back in town I was asked if I would interview Dr. Tillich in front of the conference audience. I agreed because I felt if I could draw out Paul Tillich the person this would probably be greatly appreciated by the conference members. This interview in front of a large audience was far from being a success by my standards. Dr. Tillich had excellent statements to make to each of the questions that I asked or in regard to the comments I made. However, each of the statements that he may made seemed highly abstract as though drawn from some reservoir of speeches or essays which he had presented in the past.

My reaction to the interview was well summed up by a member of our staff who said to me afterwards, in a somewhat mournful tone, 'Well, that was a good try Carl.'

The next day San Diego State asked if Dr. Tillich and I would converse with one another in front of TV cameras. I determined that I would divert to make it more of a dialogue hoping to us to draw them out more. I felt that these two dialogues were much more successful. And some of the significant personal points of view of each of us, I think, are contained in the two have our conversations which we held. "Carl Rogers followed this with a few comments on technical aspects of the TV interviews. There appeared to be no particular material relative to either Carl Rogers's or Paul Tillich's theories.

Rogers did take note that Paul Tillich died a few months later and the interview was his last public appearance.

Personal Comments on the Lost Introduction

It is well known that the person-centered approach with Carl Rogers being the premier articulator of the approach has held several premises: unconditional positive regard, nondirectiveness, and nonjudgmentalness.

It occurred to me as I listened to Carl Rogers' introduction that he held the reputation of Paul Tillich in high esteem. After all, agree or disagree with him personally, Paul Tillich had a major impact on Theology and Philosophy before and after World War II. This influence continues into the new millennium.

Rogers though abandoned the principle of nondirectiveness for this interview. He said, "I felt if I could draw out Paul Tillich the person this would probably be greatly appreciated by the conference members." I found myself believing that the genuine Carl Rogers attempted to "draw out" someone. Yet, this contradicted my perception of his commitment to nondirectiveness. That doesn't mean he was committed to it in his personal and professional interactions. My own observations via media was that he lived the approach, not just talked it. I am surprised by his commitment to "draw out" Tillich for the people engaged in listening to the dialogue.

Rogers in this drawing out also seemed patronizing to me even has he appeared to respect Tillich's reputation. Paul Tillich was a public figure who rubbed shoulders with the likes of Karl Barth, Rudolf Bultmann, Reinhold Niebuhr, and a host of others. He had lectured and preached in uncounted settings. It is doubtful that Carl Rogers needed to draw him out. Rogers's position essentially says that Tillich withheld himself from audiences. How one would determine that is far more complicated than one or two public interviews. I found myself seeing Rogers as presumptuous here.

I am not a fan of nondirectiveness, but I at least appreciated the stance that Rogers had on maintaining it. I wonder though why apparently, he was not, nor are many of his followers willing to apply this kind of directiveness to clients. Do they feel they violate clients, but not people like Paul Tillich when they behave this way? I would think it would be the opposite. One would facilitate the drawing out of clients but enjoy the genuineness of the widely respected person.

In addition, Rogers struck me presupposing that the audience would appreciate his efforts to draw out Tillich. Allegedly the venue was full of interested people. People had come to hear Paul Tillich earlier, and then Carl Rogers and Paul Tillich. In a sense, to be in the auditorium would have been an awesome experience. It would not be surprising with that many people that there would have been those who were disappointed. They might have been disappointed in Tillich, or Rogers, or Rogers's effort to draw out Tillich, or both men. However, surely, there were those who were very pleased.

This leads me to the next violation of the approach, the violation of the premise of nonjudgmentalness. Rogers said in his introduction, "each of the statements that he may made seemed highly abstract as though drawn from some reservoir of speeches or essays which he had presented in the past." The judgmentalness was in the implication that Tillich should have been far less abstract. He had no history of being less abstract. I have seen nothing by Tillich that was not loaded with abstraction save for sermons (Fant, C. E., & Pinson Jr, W., 1971). The deviation from Rogers's stance on nonjudgmentalness shows up in the following statement. "My reaction to the interview was well summed up by a member of our staff who said to me afterwards, in a somewhat mournful tone, well, that was a good try Carl." I do not a clue what "well, that was a good try Carl" means. It reeked with disappointment from these advocates of nonjudgmentalness. I found myself wondering what Rogers and this staff member were looking for. I know I was looking for consistency. I was looking for seeing and hearing and interaction between to giants in their fields. I got that. I have to say, I also was disappointed, which is seen in my grousing here.

I have not seen a lot of evidence pointing to Carl Rogers having read much of Paul Tillich's material. His own material never triggered in me an "ah, Tillich said something like that." Nor, did I see any evidence that Rogers attended presentations, lectures, or sermons by Paul Tillich. Thus, I personally experienced a sense of Rogers's judgmentalness about Tillich being abstract. I missed empathic responses and knowledgeable responses about Tillich's frame of reference. So, my sense is, what you see is what you get. The drawn-out Tillich is an abstract thinker. Rogers was successful and did not know it.

Hereto, I do not have a lot of room for nonjudgmentalness and consistently find myself hoping and wishing that adherents would stop using the term. However, it is doubtful it will disappear.

I am though satisfied that Carl Rogers had profound respect for Paul Tillich. This respect transcended the directiveness and judgmentalness I felt I saw from Rogers. However, I am not prepared to say this was unconditional positive regard. Would Carl Rogers have been willing to meet with others for such a dialogue who did not have the reputation of Tillich? Certainly, he did so for demonstration purposes many times. Just as certain, there was only so much of Carl Rogers to go around, thus limiting his personal ability to offer positive regard to people anyway. The willingness could extend only so far. Therefore, Tillich was an easy top list priority. I would not have been.

I submit that unconditional positive regard is so limited that it is no longer useful. Accepting what one can, the way one can do so, must be sufficient, regardless of regard (Bower, 2011).

I am viewing two persons of great reputations who had a moment in history together. Their reputations made it special. Their presence, their capabilities, and their talents made their reputations possible.

In the scheme of things, only a tiny percentage of people even wanted to visit this event where two intellectual giants came together. Even fewer even made that visit, with even fewer remembering what was said. Some of us will enjoy the awe and wonder of their meeting, which may include not liking what the interaction and being disappointed.

I for one feel I saw a side of Carl Rogers that was not congruent with his premises. I saw a genuine Carl Rogers whom I felt was judgmental. I also felt I saw a genuine Paul Tillich. I don't believe that "Well, that was a good try Carl" captured anything but disappointment. Paul Tillich gave us Paul Tillich.

Now the Hard Part: Gleaning Through the Tillich-Rogers Dialogue

The dialogue is available elsewhere (Kirshenbaum, & Henderson, 1989), among other sources. Therefore, I want to get at my thoughts and experiences as I go through the material for the first time. This is consistent with the way I approach material. I trust my responses, especially the errors. I learn something. I find that these often trigger responses in others, even if that response is to tell me how incorrect I am. I also trust the interpretations I have for they may facilitate different interpretations in others.

I predict, since I am writing this section before I explore the formal Tillich-Rogers dialogue, that I will not be able to present all the material I want to present. The dialogue probably has far too many points to address.

In addition, I must take into consideration that both Rogers and Tillich probably said things I won't understand. There simply will be too much complexity for me to deal with.

They also probably said things that I won't even consider worth commenting on.

The reproduction of the dialogue will encumber this article. My source for that dialogue will be the one reproduced in (Kirschenbaum & Henderson, 1989).

It also offers an annotated version of the Rogers-Tillich Dialogue in another chapter.

References

Bower, D. W. (2011). *Revising the person-centered approach: Pushing on the envelope, but not very hard.* Bloomington, iUniverse.

Cooper, T. D. (2006). *Paul Tillich and psychology: historic and contemporary explorations in theology, psychotherapy, and ethics.* Macon, GA: Mercer University Press.

Corey, G. (1982). *Theory and practice of counseling and psychotherapy.* Monterey, CA: Brooks/Cole Publishing Company.

Fant, C. E., & Pinson Jr, W. (1971). *20 Centuries of Great Preaching: An Encyclopedia of Preaching*, 13 Volumes. Waco: Word Books.

Kahler, M. (1964). *The so-called historical Jesus and the historic biblical Christ* (C. E. Graaten, Trans., Ed.). Philadelphia, Fortress Press.

Kirschenbaum, H., & Henderson, V. L. (1989). *Carl Rogers dialogues.* Boston: Houghton Mifflin.

May, R. (1973). *Paulus: Reminiscences of a friendship.* New York: HarperCollins Publishers.

Rogers, C., & Tillich, P. (2006). Carl Rogers and Paul Tillich #1 & - (1960) Rogers and theologian Paul Tillich. San Francisco: Saybrook Graduate School & Research Center. http://www.carlrogers.info/video.html

Schwietzer, A. (2005). *The quest for the historical Jesus* (W. Montgomery, Trans.). New York: Dover Publications.

Tillich, P. (1967). *Systematic theology: Three volumes in one.* Chicago: The University of Chicago Press.

Awkwardly Exploring The Paul Tillich - Carl Rogers Dialogue:

A Critical Exploration

(Part A)

<u>What I Observed (Or How I Responded)</u>

Rogers opened the dialogue by speaking to "self-affirmation" and "the courage to be." He asserted that the two concepts held some commonality. As a naive reader imagining that I was in the audience, I found myself already uninformed. What is self-affirmation? What is the courage to be? How are they the same? I experienced ignorance. Is the concept of self-affirmation presented by a humanist (if I dare place Rogers into that arena), consistent with the concept of the courage to be presented an existentialist? I heard no exploration of the concepts. Thus, the comparison was beyond my grasp.

I also did not understand what Rogers meant by the terms "logical positivistic," "ultra-scientific approach," "mechanistic," and "deterministic." I didn't learn what they meant for Rogers or Tillich.

However, I did feel that the heart of his concerns with the above terms was the dehumanization of human beings. The human being is just an object under these perceptions. Rogers and Tillich both had a concern about that.

While, I am not a fan of the Rogerian term "nondirective," I believe that the term is indeed about empowering people and thus respect the humanity through respecting the potentials of human beings to resolve their own problems. Where I feel the term falls short is the person coming to another for help is seeking to expand his or her own resources to deal with his/her personal world (Bower, 2011). In short, the client coming to another for therapy, may indeed be seeking fresh ideas and has the capability of rejecting any or all of those fresh ideas regarding finding resolution for person problems. A strict adherence to nondirectiveness will withhold therapist advice and feedback (Rogers, 1951, 1961, 1980).

Tillich essentially concurred with Rogers about the agreement. However, I did not learn from Tillich what the concepts above meant to him. Tillich (2000) presented the two concepts ("self-affirmation" and "courage to be") together. A major theme of the original work, as (Schilken, 1997) noted was, "courage is the strength to continue to live on in a meaningful way in spite of the fact that our existence appears to have no purpose. We do not wallow in doubt, self-derision or despair. We have come into being in this time, in this place, in spite of the ever-present threat of non-being." Would this be congruent with the concept of self-actualization? Somehow, the person drawing on personal resources thrives via a host of psychological, social, and yes spiritual levels to both exist and function as a unique person among other unique persons. The "Overview" (Google, 2009) of Tillich's (2000) work asserts the work, "describes the dilemma of modern man and points a way to the conquest of the problem of anxiety."

Tillich's own (2000) comments are in relationship to Spinoza's version of humanism, not Rogers's. That focus does not have the positive slant that Rogers has of the human situation. I learned early from Corey (1982) that Rogers's= view of human nature is a positive one. Tillich's view is about angst.

Thus, the agreement stated by Tillich escapes me. I am not convinced that the self-affirmation of Rogers equals the courage to be of Tillich. In fact, Tillich wrote, "Modern humanism is still humanism, rejecting the idea of salvation. But modern humanism also rejects renunciation" (p. 19). Indeed, with Rogers (1986), there is no need for salvation, but renunciation runs counter to the concept of nonjudgmentalness and unconditional positive regard. Rogers then would be consistent with Tillich's description of Spinoza's position. If in this description we see Tillich's position, then Rogers and Tillich are in agreement. However, it is not reflective of Tillich's position who speaks about issues of estrangement. If one is estranged, there is room for some wort of salvation, internal or external in relationship to that estrangement. Tillich has some room for renunciation that humanism does not share. Rogers's humanism is not reflective of Tillich's position who speaks about issues of estrangement. If one is estranged, there is room for some sort of salvation, internal or external in relationship to that estrangement. If renunciation of the condition of estrangement is confronting it, then Tillich and Rogers are not in the same frame of ideals.

Assuming that there was agreement Rogers moves in another direction. There is nothing like agreement to stifle interaction.

Rogers moved to explore his own uncertainties.

He sought to deal with the "nature of man." He did so in part by extending a query to Tillich about his perspective on the issue. Quickly, Rogers presented a presupposition that existentialists hold that "man" has no nature.

Such a position never occurred to me. Can the human being who has fallen into existence, engages or avoids angst, and is considered an ontological entity, not have a nature? Can there by existentialism without ontology, even if there are disagreements or contradictions in expressing thoughts, ideas, and presuppositions? Thus, can existentialism assert that man has not nature?

Rogers then spoke of his view that man belongs to specific species and shares the characteristics of those species. I note in this that we share characteristics with gorillas, apes, and other primates. One can find it difficult to point to what makes human beings so different from these other creatures.

While not at all intending to speak to this, Rogers asserts that man tends to move towards actualizing one's self. However, animals do so as well. We just don't speak of animals as creatures that self-actualize. Yet, in this Rogers asserted that man's nature can be describable.

Rogers then wanted to explore Tillich's position on "demonic aspects of man." Rogers held the goodness of man. With this, I felt Tillich was being baited. It is well known that Rogers held the goodness of man. My own exposure to that came with Corey (1982). It was reinforced uncounted times during my personal pilgrimage with the person-centered approach. One of my favorite sources of this was a Rogers (1986) article in which he highlighted differences regarding the person-centered approach and other orientations such as Christianity, and psychoanalytic theory.

Tillich (1967) had room for a more negative view of human nature. He had a positive view as well. Rogers was either naive, or insincere in his query. It is doubtful that any follower of Rogers would think he was insincere. I think I would have felt differently about this section had Rogers spoke of his view of the "nature of man" and then inquired about Tillich's. The contrast would quickly be revealed. Instead, I felt one had to already be familiar with Rogers' position.

In Tillich's response to Rogers, he quickly affirmed the existence of the "nature" of man. While he pointed to Sartre as an existentialist who denied that man has a nature, Tillich asserted that man's freedom to "make himself" is itself a nature. Tillich thus denied that one could deny the nature of man.

Tillich stated that he perceives two natures in man. The first is his true or essential nature. He moved theologically towards presenting this true nature as a created nature. This nature was created "good." He supported that from the creation epic of the first chapter of Genesis. He also supported the theological position by drawing from Augustine.

Tillich acknowledged the controversy in the early Church over this issue. I was personally surprised that he limited that acknowledgment to the early Church since the issue continues. Perhaps he did so because there is such a strong emphasis on the depravity of man which is marked by sin characterized by corruption, vanity, and personal or spiritual poverty among other descriptions (Calvin, 1960). This issue of goodness is accepted in the contemporary Church and lead to Rogers (1986) comments.

The negative stance may cover Tillich's affirmation of the true nature of man being good. Here Rogers's= position and Tillich's agree. It probably is safe to say that the congruent person is fundamentally good. It may also be safe to say that this is true of the incongruent person. That person's basic nature is good. The distortion of that however, leads to a myriad of issues. I am sure one of them is the state of incongruence, which blocks awareness of the person's experiences and personal condition.

Tillich though ventures to the second nature (an existential nature) as "mixed." This mix is the "accepting" and the "distorting" of one's true nature. Man finds the self as estranged from one's true nature. Man contradicts the true nature. For Tillich, this nature is very human and without it, man would not be man. However, as real as it is, Tillich saw it as a distortion of the essential nature.

I found myself wondering though if this existential nature was absent, would the human being in a state of total essential nature be human. While this is an ideal state, surely the human being could be fully the self that one truly is without the mix that Tillich presented. That may be part of Tillich's position. The real person, the real human presently has this "mix" as part of the nature of man and cannot escape it.

This position seems in accord with Roger's concept of incongruence.

In the dialogue, Tillich offered to go into a third position. However, Rogers again entered the dialogue moving from listener to presenter. Personally, if I wait to make a point, I forget what I responding to, or what my point is. I must act on my thoughts and experiences during interactions before they get away from me. I do not know if that is what happened with Rogers.

Rogers expressed what has become one of my favorite stances in the person-centered approach. In my words, it is the position of being open to whatever the direction the client takes. Rogers holds that in this openness rather than the client choosing to move in "evil" or "antisocial" ways, the client moves in directions of "self-understanding" and "more social behavior."

On this aspect, though I like the stance, I do not agree. I found people getting in touch with their despair, anger, ability to be hurtful and harmful, and anxiety. I remember one of my mentors asserting that the child abuser might become a better child abuser under this framework. I found this troubling. I am personally not interested in facilitating a person's path to finding creative and resourceful ways to hurting others.

Instead, I found myself taking a position of being open to the possibility that a client may indeed move in "evil" or "antisocial" ways. Yet, I also found that with continuous or consistent offerings of the core conditions of empathy, acceptance, and genuineness, the client was more likely to move in the directions that Rogers addressed.

I am convinced that the absence of the "core conditions" is more likely to foster "antisocial" and "self-destructive" behaviors (Bower, 2000). This is more serious than whether the "core conditions" facilitate constructive and productive actualization processes.

Rogers essentially addressed the issue of freedom whereby the therapist creates an environment of freedom being open the self-directiveness. "We may say that the counselor chooses to act consistently upon the hypothesis that the individual has a sufficient capacity to deal constructively with all those aspects of his life which can potentially come into conscious awareness. This means the creation of an interpersonal situation in which material may come into the client's awareness, and a meaningful demonstration of the counselor's acceptance of the client as a person who is competent to direct himself" (Rogers, 1951, p. 14).

Tillich though questioned whether a person is free enough to create such an environment. He thus appeared not to have a place for what Rogers would call congruence. The existential person is in a constant state of alienation from the self and wouldn't be able to escape enough from that state to enter such freedom. If the therapist isn't really free to be fully the essential nature, how could he/she be free to create freedom for another. This is an important distinction and a difficult question for the person-centered approach. In fact, despite the alleged goodness of human beings, there are constant reports of bad behavior. If human beings are so good, how do we talk about them acting so badly? We can blame society for failing to offer the conditions Rogers asserted were necessary and sufficient to facilitate personal growth and change. But doesn't that take responsibility away from the person for his or her bad behavior. We could also question what bad behavior is. In this, anything goes.

In this, Tillich spoke to the "ambiguity of life." This ambiguity arises out of the dichotomy of the essential nature and the existential nature. Perhaps, to say it arises out of the tension between the self that one truly is, and the distorted self might capture some aspect of the ambiguous. The tension captured by Tillich would at least seem to address the notorious destructive and self-destructive behaviors found in the realm of being human behavior. Rogers's position on the goodness of humankind may give an account of the resourceful and creative aspects of human behavior. It does not do so well when speaking about the horrors and atrocities committed by human beings. He was not naïve about those atrocities (Rogers, 1961).

> I experienced myself wondering, first, how marvelous it is that Paul Tillich being a man of profound reputation, of equal reputation in a differing field, in relationship to Carl Rogers, was able to raise issue with Rogers on the issue of freedom. Over the years I acquiesced to the giants in my life and did not feel comfortable with questioning their position

Then second, I wondered if the use of the word freedom was a distraction on the issue of creating an environment that Rogers has long espoused. Is being open to the direction a client takes really about freedom? Perhaps being open to those directions are about legalism from time to time. Good person-centered therapists are open to the direction that clients may take. One is supposed to behave in such a manner. That does not sound like freedom, but obligation. Yet, it is not presented as a necessary and sufficient condition. Thus, concern about legalism is not well founded. It is then an observation. When therapists are open to the directions of clients (negative or positive), the clients tend to move in constructive directions. It does not mean they will.

Tillich saw this "predicament" as universal. He thus, differs from presuppositions of Rogers about the nature of man as Rogers does have room for a fully functioning person (Rogers, 1961). Tillich's position has a great deal of room for evil. Tillich (1967) may have, in some way, spoken about this in relationship to his concept of "new being." However, neither person addressed these concepts at this point in the dialogue. However, Tillich stated, "so I am more skeptical, both about the creation of such a situation and about the individuals who are in such a situation" (pp. 68).

I think this supports that unfortunate use of the word freedom by Rogers. As above, it is probably more of an issue of being open to the directions the client may take. This then would be, or could be, conceived as a freedom to get at the human predicament any client is experiencing. Therefore, the word "freedom" may not be so unfortunate as to not use it all. Perhaps freedom is really freedom when one is free to be broken. However, if a person is broken, can that person have the freedom to no longer be broken? Can deep brokenness be overcome? If so, why is not overcome readily?

Rogers augmented his position a bit acknowledging that creating an environment of "complete freedom" was difficult. However, he did not back away from his belief that a person in an environment of acceptance and understanding seems "to liberate the person to move toward really social goals" (p. 68).

Rogers then inquired about Tillich's position on the demonic.

Tillich first addressed where he felt there was some agreement with Rogers. He saw some importance for love in the formative years of children. However, he left a very interesting question unanswered. "Where are the forces which create a situation in which the child receives that love which gives him, later on, the freedom to face life and not to escape from life into neurosis and psychoses?" (p. 69).

For me, I revisited my believing that the absence of love, or in the case of the person-centered approach, the absence of the core conditions, is all too real in life. The escape into neurosis and psychoses relates to that absence (Bower, 2000).

Tillich then makes a brief dive into his concept of the demonic. In doing so, he spoke of his contact with the psychoanalytic movement in the 1920s and its impact on "changing the climate of the whole century" (p. 69). It would be interesting if he had developed what that change was about in this section of his dialogue.

He also addressed briefly the impact of Karl Marx but did not elaborate on that impact either. In this, he asserted that traditional concepts of the "fallen" or "sinful" nature of man were somehow inadequate to address the changes in relationship to Freud and Marx.

Personally, I felt this showed his bias because I have no trouble myself using those terms in relationship to either Freud or Marx: with Freud, because his assertions concerning the "Id" which has an aspect of selfishness, greed, and self-centeredness; and with Marx, because of his assertions concerning oppression and domination by the elite social classes over the lower classes.

Tillich felt the term "demonic" was more appropriate. He affirmed its connection with New Testament stories of Jesus. It was "similar" to being possessed (p. 69). There is something within the individual that interferes acting in "good will." In this, he denied a mythological component: "little demons or a personal Satan running around the world" (p. 69). Rather, this demonic is ambiguous, destructive, and is part of the estrangement of humankind. The demonic takes hold of a person leading to conflicts in class, and society. Even efforts to overcome them seem to drive people deeper into the demonic.

Rogers responded to the issues of alienation and estrangement by utilizing infants as an illustration. He asserted that an infant is not estranged from him or herself.

I agree and disagree with Rogers. I have long trusted that when an infant was crying it was crying-out in sync with itself. There is something wrong. When an infant is cooing, it is in sync with itself. The infant is content.

However, I disagree in the sense that a cry out of hunger sounds the same as a cry about pain in the foot. The estrangement from the self rests in not yet being able to access the way to accurately communicate what it needs. Further, there is estrangement from others. The infant moved from a nice warm wet environment, into a bright, maybe colder, dry environment. Sounds are different. Experiences are different. The infant can even make his/her own sounds. In short, the infant is in process of discovering how to function and is often out of touch with how to stop crying when conditions change. I am convinced that infants might be able to stop cooing quicker than they can stop crying.

Rogers continued speaking to the infant's path towards adulthood and his/her encounter with the significant others, probably parents, in regard to love, judgments, and other psycho-social experiences.

I found it interesting that Rogers used the term "bad boy, bad boy" in his dialogue on these issues. Rogers illustrates this, "In other words, he has introjected the notion that he is bad, where actually his enjoying the experience . . ." (p. 70). This of course assumes that he is enjoying the experience. What happens if as he enjoys such experiences, he hits a little girl when he gets older? What if he appears to be enjoying an experience, but it is a misinterpretation by Rogers that the experience is satisfying? There appears to me to be a glimpse of the issue of nonjudgmentalness in Rogers's take here. Yet, it also appears to me to be a glimpse at the cause of estrangement from one's self, which is also part of the Rogerian position. That is, if the person is basically good, it remains that the boy hit the girl. Can this be representative of being "basically good?" If the enjoyment of the boy hitting girl does not reflect the boy's basic goodness, he is incongruent. In addition, the basically good boy violated the girl's space even as the boy enjoys it. The boy enjoying his own behavior may be part of the violation of both his basic goodness and the girl's right to be treated with respect. Rogers scantly dealt with this incongruence.

Could it be though that a person raised in a nonjudgmental environment, if that were possible, might have his/her own kind of estrangement and incongruence? I would assert yes. If the basic tendency of the person is good and that person strikes out at others in name of self-actualizing, the other person involved is violated. The goodness in such behavior is lost.

In response, Tillich states "the infant is a very important problem" (Kirschenbaum & Henderson, 1989, p. 70). He compared the infant to Adam and Eve before the Fall. He called this "dreaming innocence." The reality of the infant's being has "not yet reached reality." Tillich noted that "the Fall" does not reflect as closely this state of dreaming innocence as does this psychological jargon. For

Tillich, the dreaming innocence of the infant and the Fall mean the same. For him there is a process of movement away from dreaming innocence or the Fall to "conscious self-actualization." In the midst of this, estrangement occurs.

At this point, I agreed with Tillich. He said to Rogers, "I agree with you that there is also in what the parents used to call "bad boy" or "bad girl," there is a necessary act of self-fulfillment, but there is also something asocial in it, because it hurts his sister and so it has to be repressed, and whether we say, "bad boy" or prevent it in anyway, this is equally necessary . . ." (pp. 70-71).

Certainly, Rogers is correct. There is a thwarting of the self in this act. Yet, Tillich is also correct. Hurting another person is unacceptable. There is room for the resistance of a society that frowns on or prevents hurting others. If saying "bad boy" or "bad girl" can prevent that is that reasonable even under the concept of nonjudgmentalness? Tillich recognized the tension in the movement from dreaming innocence to self-actualization as well as the estrangement that occurs.

This does not strike me as consistent with Rogers who espouses that a nonjudgmental stance liberates the person towards more social behavior. As much as I agree an environment can help facilitate movement towards more social behavior, I also resist the notion in part because I believe there is the possibility of a laissez faire attitude that could also facilitate asocial behavior. Rogers (1951) did not condone laissez faire behavior. My own impression of the approach in general is laissez faire may be deliberately or non-deliberately advocated in the staunch nonjudgmental emphasis of the approach.

Rogers began a response by saying, "there is much that I would agree with" (Kirschenbaum & Henderson, 1989, p. 71). It would be great to a sense of where he thought the agreement was. I personally think there is agreement with the Rogers concept of incongruence, and Tillich's concept of estrangement. However, Tillich, as noted above, is not as optimistic about the overcoming of estrangement. Rogers is optimistic about the overcoming of incongruence.

Certainly, anyone dealing with the interview could state where he or she thought agreement rested, but I did not see it. What I am missing is where Rogers thought the agreement was.

Rogers moved from this brief statement to what he believes bring healing to the estranged incongruent human person. In Rogers's position, this is estrangement from the self. The "courage to be" or the "tendency to become oneself" for Rogers is seen as occurring only in a relationship. He asserted that acceptance of the unacceptable aspects of oneself can only occur in an accepting relationship. This statement triggered a connection with my understanding of Rogers (1957) hypothesis on the "necessary and sufficient conditions" for therapeutic change.

Rogers said, "This, I think, is a large share of what constitutes psychotherapy - that the individual finds that the feelings he has been ashamed of or that he has been unable to admit into his awareness, that those can be accepted by another person, so then he becomes able to accept them as part of himself" (Kirschenbaum & Henderson, 1989, p. 71).

An aspect of acceptance remains unclear to me. Does acceptance amount to condoning of previously seen as immoral, asocial or antisocial behavior? For instance, does the discovery that a person abuses children become acceptable? If the person is doing the best he or she can do, is child abuse acceptable? I have been in dialogues with person-centered colleagues who appeared to me to condone the child abuse. Fortunately, I have not seen such affirmations in the literature I have explored. However, on the personal level charges of being judgmental have been levied towards people who expressed concern about a person abusing children. I myself, find I am willing for a client to speak to the issue of abusing children. I am unwilling to give the impression that I condone child abuse or other antisocial behavior.

Tillich affirmed Rogers's stance on the importance of acceptance as "necessary" for "self-affirmation." He added the word "forgiveness" to this acceptance. Forgiveness though in the person-centered approach is not necessary, since the person is basically good. It would only be necessary if a person feels violated by another person and chooses not to carry the feelings, thoughts, and experiences that go with feeling violated. As a therapist, I do not need to offer the client forgiveness.

This helped me add a new twist to my concept of "forgiveness." I have traditionally viewed the concept as a setting aside of the consequences regarding personal, moral, ethical, or legal violations. A person might overlook the insult of a friend or another person instead of lashing back. Alternatively, a judge might decide, based on evidence and circumstances, to drop charges with the cooperation of the prosecution. The strong Biblical flavor of forgiveness is to forget the violation. A more realistic Biblical flavor of forgiveness is not to impose judgment on the person committing the violation. It is hardly realistic to ask people to forget as part of forgiveness.

What Tillich added for me was seeing forgiveness as "acceptance of the unacceptable." He didn't indicate the unacceptable becomes acceptable.

I thought though I heard Tillich say that one cannot accept oneself. This does not come out in the written dialogue recording by (Kirschenbaum & Henderson, p. 71). Rather, it came for listening to a recording I have of the tape. This is not to say it is impossible. It seems related to a proneness "to hate yourself." As long as that self-hate exists, it diminishes then the ability to forgive oneself.

Here Tillich differs from Rogers who asserts this acceptance is about relationship. For Tillich holds the formal confessional rites of the Church, and probably other institutions, are important for something of "another dimension." Still, Tillich affirms that a relationship "from men to men" makes acceptance within the confessional rites possible.

Tillich though stated that he all but abandoned the use of forgiveness in this context "because this often produces a bad superiority in him who forgives and the humiliation of him who is forgiven" (Kirschenbaum & Henderson, pp. 71-72). I would assert though that should this be the case, this is not forgiveness. It is patronization. Forgiveness levels the "playing field," if I may use a common term. It creates equality, not disparity. One releases the attitude of superiority and also inferiority, "how dare they treat me like that." Harboring ill will or bad feelings towards or about another is removed.

Tillich acknowledged that he preferred the word "acceptance." He saw it a very adequate term to update old presuppositions concerning forgiveness. Here he probably matches well with Rogers's concept of unconditional positive regard: "the way in which the psychoanalyst accepts his patients, no judging him, not telling him first he should be good, otherwise I cannot accept you, but accepting him just because he is not good, but he has something within himself that wants to be good (p. 72).

The use of the word "psychoanalyst" may indicate Tillich's limitation on what "psychotherapy" is about. Rogers (1986) position is hardly that affirming of the psychoanalytic perspective since he sees it as the psychoanalyst assuming the role of expert and thus creating the very attitude of superiority that Tillich was concerned about in relationship to the concept of forgiveness.

I doubt very seriously if the concept of acceptance really is so immune to Tillich's concern about forgiveness. Surely, acceptance can come with this issue of superiority. That's is a person can still not only say, look at me how forgiving I am, but can also say, look at me how accepting I am. It just struck me that the concept of unconditional positive regard can have its humanistic grandeur.

Rogers responded by asserting strongly his belief in acceptance. Here he noted that the "potency of acceptance" is demonstrated "when an individual feels that he is both fully accepted in all that he has been able to express and yet prized as a person."

My own explorations and experiences in the approach hold experientially that this holds true. However, I want to push it beyond prizing and positive regard. Can I accept the "negative?" Can I be open to my own experiences of negativity with the client, not necessary overtly expressing them, but taking note of them for what they are? Can I incorporate feelings of dismay, frustration, even anger, into the perceptions I have in relationship to another? Can I trust these experiences regardless of regard, positive, neutral, or negative? Does such a position offer its own kinds of challenge? Is it freer of being grandiose because if the therapist struggles to accept the client regardless of regard, there is nothing about which to be grandiose? The acceptance can suddenly disappear.

Is acceptance romanticized when associated with warm fuzzy experiences romanticized? When the therapist believes in the person no matter what the person does, has the therapist rationalized acceptance?

Tillich responded to Rogers's notion of acceptance by stating that this acceptance is at the heart of the "good news" of the Christian message. While this isn't foreign to Rogers's own pilgrimage, it is foreign to the message of the person-centered approach. Certainly, the traditional Christian song "Just as I am" confirms Tillich's assertion. It seems, at least on the surface, to be compatible with Rogers's concept of acceptance.

Hereto the Christian message suffers from the same possibilities. It can be perceived so radically, and then when the acceptance it espouses is not present, the Christian faith comes into question. One might offer charges of Christians are hypocrites.

Is acceptance always a pleasant positive experience? Can there be room for accepting that it feels awful to be human at times? Does acceptance as a person of feel unpleasant at times? How about therapists accepting clients? Surely, clients have experiences of feeling awful, and their therapists feel awful about them. Is there room to include this in the manifestation of acceptance? Pushing it even further, is there room to accept "unacceptability?"

At this point in the dialogue, there was break or "Intermission." I find myself staggered by the material addressed so far and wondering can it hold together.

References

Bower, D. W. (2000). *The person-centered approach: Applications for living.* San Jose, CA: Writers Club Press.

Bower, D. W. (2011). *Revising the person-centered approach: Pushing on the envelope, but not very hard.* Bloomington, iUniverse.

Corey, G. (1982). *Theory and practice of counseling and psychotherapy.* Monterey, CA: Brooks/Cole Publishing Company.

Google (2009). *Overview: The courage to be.* http://books.google.com/books?id=xnw6zW2MXNgC&dq= inauthor:Paul+inauthor:Tillich&lr=&as_drrb_is=q&as_minm_ is=0&as_miny_is=&as_maxm_is=0&as_maxy_is=&as_ brr=0&source=gbs_navlinks_s.

Kirschenbaum, H., & Henderson, V. L. (1989). *Carl Rogers dialogues.* Boston: Houghton Mifflin.

Rogers, C. R. (1951). *Client-centered therapy.* Boston: Houghton Mifflin.

Rogers, C. R. (1961). *On becoming a person.* Boston: Houghton Mifflin.

Rogers, C. R. (1980). *A way of being.* Boston: Houghton Mifflin.

Rogers, C. R. (1986). Rogers, Kohut, and Erickson: A personal perspective and some similarities and difference. *Person-Centered Review,* 1(2), 125-140.

Schilken, R. (1997). Book Review: The Courage To Be by Paul Tillich. Retrieved from blogcritics.org/book-review-the-courage-to-be/

Tillich, P. (1967). *Systematic theology: Three volumes in one.* Chicago: The University of Chicago Press.

Tillich, P. (2000). *The courage to be.* (The Terry Lectures Series). New Haven: Yale University Press. Kindle Edition.

Awkwardly- Exploring The Paul Tillich - Carl Rogers Dialogue:

A Critical Exploration

(Part B)

When a double header takes place in baseball, the second game is usually different from the first game. Therefore, before approaching the second half of this dialogue I quickly wondered what might be different. I tried not to anticipate what would be different, only that it might be different.

Tillich kicked off the second session by speaking about the minister as a representative of "the ultimate meaning of life." There was no development of what that meant. Without that development, one can only wonder.

He linked this with the "unconscious skills" of this minister. While having skills, the minister, being "unskilled" should not attempt to be a "second rate psychotherapist." This is unclear. However, since Tillich referred to Freud earlier, I do not find it farfetched to think he had psychoanalysis in mind. If this was true, I wondered how much psychotherapy at the time was associated with psychoanalysis and thus biased his view. Certainly, I agree that untrained people should not be psychotherapists in any discipline of psychotherapy. However, there is more helping taking place in the world that leads to productive change than takes place in psychotherapy. If not, the world is in worse shape than we can imagine. There are not enough psychotherapists within all the disciplines to be of help. Other forms of help are essential. I would Tillich may have had in mind those skills of the minister.

Regarding presuppositions related to what constitutes therapy, Rogers demythologized psychotherapy and counseling. That in part may have been why he had such severe critics, he was not speaking their language (Kirschenbaum, 1979). The conditions he espoused as therapeutic are found in some neat people in the world who are teachers, grandparents, priests, nurses, etc. I left convinced after reading Rogers (1939, & 1942) that he was influenced by such people. If therapy as described by Rogers (empathy, acceptance, and genuineness) is the restructuring of the self (Rogers, 1961), then restructuring might take place in a synagogue, school classroom, on a walk in a park, or in a hospital room. It cannot be limited to the domain of Psychoanalytic, Gestalt, Cognitive Behavioral, or Person-Centered therapy. There are those who take exception to this believing it is a professional discipline practiced only by those with specific training. Tillich it would seem was one of them. I do not believe I am contradicting myself on this issue of training. I am simply asserting that restructuring of personality is not the goal of all helping and healing. Certainly, those with who focus on the practice of offering formal counseling, psychiatry, or psychotherapy need licensure. However, restructuring of the self has to occur outside of psychotherapy as change is built into human behavior, though all too often thwarted.

When Rogers responded I saw something of him that I long suspected but couldn't quite put my finger on. That is, he grew up in a traditionalist, fundamental Congregationalist household. He made a trip to China in that mindset that changed his life and his theology. I have long felt that his position was essentially secular Christianity. However, humanism also powerfully influenced him. In this, he felt that discarding traditional Christian language would be very appropriate. I have no way of knowing if Rogers discarded his faith with discarding the Christian jargon. Rogers said to Tillich: "I realize very well that I and many other therapists are interested in the kind of issues that involved the religious worker and the theologian, and yet, for myself, I prefer to put my thinking on those issues in humanistic terms, or to attack those issues through the channels of scientific investigation" (Kirschenbaum & Henderson, 1989, p. 72).

A Negative Personal Reflection

While studying at Southern Baptist Theological Seminary in Louisville, KY, I took a nursing position in a local hospital. There I got the first taste that there were psychotherapists who blamed religion as a major cause of mental illness. The statements I heard seemed dismissive and discounted the realm of faith. The person-centered approach despite Rogers's attitude above has hardly been friendly towards people of faith. I have seen some intense mean-spirited discussions in person-centered community meetings about religion. I among others learned to keep my mouth shut about some of my traditional values as a person of faith.

Still, personally, I appreciate Rogers's position on this. I didn't like his apparent denial about the negative side of behavior and have a lot of room for saying theologically, we are sinners in need of God's love and redemption. However, this work is not a theological treatise or a defense of traditional Christianity. I did find that Rogers insistence on the goodness of humans was pervasive, though I have interacted with colleagues who said that comes from a misunderstanding of

Rogers. His position got me to rethink the creation narrative in Genesis with its saying, "And God saw everything that he had made, and, behold, *it was* very good. And the evening and the morning were the sixth day" Genesis 1:31 (KJV).

I have found the conditions representative of the intent of the Christian faith in particular to be of help to those who need help. I cannot think of behavior much more "Christian" than to be empathic, accepting, and genuine though there are other behaviors concerning faith not included in being person-centered. For instance, prayer, worship, scripture reading, and proclamation.

I do not feel qualified to speak about how representative of other traditions it might be.

Rogers in the interview also addressed the "God is dead" religious theme that was stirring at the time. It was apparently one the fad themes of the time that has fallen by the wayside. I have not heard it dealt with in years. I had a bumper sticker on my car about 1969 that read: "My God is not dead. Sorry about yours." I have investigated that theological position several times but have never really felt I got a handle on it. Rogers seemed to hold a notion that was like the one I did get hold of, but which I did not then and still do not appreciate. A God that dies is no God. The Jesus epic offers death and resurrection. The God is dead position offers sort of a spiritual atheism. It does also offer the rejection or abandonment of God from the hearts of people and their sophisticated societies. We need no God. I suspect this later position is closer to the position of the advocates of the God is death stance.

Rogers said to Tillich "religion no longer does speak to people in the modern world" (p. 72). He was not alone in that then, or in 2016. The likes of Borg (2001) who attempted to speak to our times, hold similar positions. The issue of irrelevancy of religion remains. Yet, D'Souza (2007) has taken note that Christianity is the fastest growing religion in the world. If he is wrong about that, I suspect that one must consider Islam as the fastest.

The claims about the irrelevance of religion are on shaky grounds. The Rogerian approach in America at least has declined as a movement, even though Rogers influenced counseling and psychotherapy more than any other humanistic theorist has. I suspect Freud probably has had more influence even if is an influence that triggers rejection of his ideas. That of course is a bias on my part. It is difficult to remove Freud, Skinner, and the Cognitive Behavioral theorists from the realms of the top spots. At any rate, Rogers had blinders on when he spoke about faith and religion in such a manner.

Rogers offered Tillich a challenging question. As to why Tillich still put his ideas in "religious terminology." Before, I attempted to find out Tillich's response, my own answer was, because Tillich did not share Rogers's view that religion no longer speaks "to people of the modern world." Tillich did use a different jargon to speak to religion and about faith. It is hardly traditional to speak of "ultimate being" for instance.

In fact, religion does speak to human beings even better than Rogers did as far as I am concerned. Even though Rogers had a significant impact, many people have never heard of him but have heard of major religions. Humanism in general has excited people, but it has also dismayed people. Of course, religion has as well. The assumption that "religion no longer speaks" to modern people was and is grossly inaccurate.

Getting back to Tillich.

Tillich pointed to what he called two metaphorical dimensions. He saw a "horizontal dimension" in which the human being connects with the self and with others. He also spoke of a "vertical" dimension in which the human connects to the "infinite, unconditional, ultimate."

The horizontal dimension is finite, limited and comes and goes. He does come close though in joining Rogers in the claim that "religion no longer speaks" to the modern person. "I don't speak here – I must emphasize this in speeches again and again – in terms of life after death, or in other symbols which cannot be used in this way anymore . . ." (p. 73). Instead, he speaks to the "immediate experience of the temporal," the temporal affected by the eternal. He saw that as a way of interpreting the "traditional religious symbols."

As an observer, I am not able to understand what Tillich meant here. I am able to understand he saw something different about his interpretation. I also feel he believed it was congruent with contemporary trends, probably around the world. I am also able to say that no matter what Tillich meant, his jargon and interpretation are hardly mainstream positions. The traditional jargon, at least of the Christian faith, strongly continues even in the face of trends that are dismissive of traditional jargon or faith (Borg, 2001; Dawkins, 2006; Harris, 2004; Hitchens, 2007; Spong, 2001). Given that we are all limited and our worldviews tend to attract the similar notions (Rogers's (1961) notion of what is most personal is most general), it is often easy to assume that any view is a common view. I certainly must apply that to what I have just said about my own observations. I do think there are a lot more regular people in the world attracted to traditional jargon about religion than there are regular people attracted to Rogers and Tillich. The Bible remains at the top of the all-time bestseller list for a reason and it does not use Rogerian, or Tillichian jargon.

Tillich though does hear that humanism as captured very succinctly in Rogers comment sees religion as "irrelevant." He thus acknowledges in his own way, what I just indicated. There are people who "live in" the traditional where there is "preaching, religious teaching, and liturgies." He felt that those "estranged" from the traditional "need a translation and interpretation of this symbol" of the traditional. However, he felt Rogers was seeking a "replacement" of the traditional. Maybe Tillich was correct in his interpretation of Rogers. However, I felt that Rogers was saying that estrangement from the traditional is not the point; rather, change was the point. The contemporary human being has moved away from even wanting the traditional and finding it inadequate for describing existing and being. Thus, self-actualization, trust of one's potentials, and moving in socially positive directions are more important to human beings.

Should I get this point accurately at all, I feel I need to point out that Rogers (1986) used this very philosophy to indicate how the person-centered approach differs from both psychoanalytic and Christian worldviews. It certainly also contrasts the flavor of contemporary forms of psychotherapies which hold the therapists as the expert (Bozarth, 1998). I tend to believe this contrast supports a position that the worldview of Christianity and other religions really has not changed so much as seen as generally irrelevant.

Tillich closed his section saying, I hope playfully, "but we poor theologians, in contrast to you happy psychologists, are in the bad situation that we know the symbols with which we deal have to be reinterpreted and even radically reinterpreted. But I have taken this heavy yoke upon myself and I have decided long ago I will continue to the end with it." Indeed, he did, He died not long after the dialogue.

That is what theology does and has done through the ages; reinterpret the faith to a new generation. Those who engage the reinterpretations sometimes embrace them and sometimes reject them as being terribly incorrect. Some find them offensive.

This too sounds like the impact of the Person-Centered Approach, which caused a stir in the psychological – psychotherapeutic arena.

Before leaving this section with its mild focus on the irrelevance of traditional religion in the contemporary world, while Rogers went to China on a missionary trip holding a traditional Christian jargon and abandoned it, Tillich though using a nontraditional jargon did not always abandon the traditional jargon (Tillich, 1955). As far as I am concerned, his sermons were quite traditional (Fant & Pinson, 1971, Vol. 10).

Rogers responded to Tillich vertical dimension with a fantasy. The vertical instead of going up, comes down. Yet, something did not quite match for me. I did not really see an up and down in Tillich's vertical dimension coming from Tillich. Rather, I simply saw a metaphor of difference. Something else felt more important to me than the up and down slant of Rogers's fantasy. Rogers spoke of being "in-tune" with the client who has come seeking help.

Of importance to me was that he used the phrase "rare moments." I have myself long held that empathic experiences are rare, sort of like peak relationship experiences where the therapist gets so focused that he/she can almost speak for the client and may even say something about the client before the client says it. In these moments Rogers described them as being occasions where operating in the therapist are forces coming together to be utilized. There seemed to me to be a flavor of awe in Rogers's statement about these rare experiences. He likened what he experienced to that scientist who can split the atom while not being the one who created the atom. He can participate in an encounter with the atom that can bring about change. The therapist does not create a client who is different but can participate in the path of the client recreating himself or herself. Something new comes from that which is old but is new by virtue of its reshaping, or its new directions, not its recreation.

Tillich however connected with the up and down aspects of Rogers comments. He pointed out that he had been accused himself of focusing on the down part of the vertical to the expense of the up part. He acknowledged that in his discussions or interest in the "ultimate concern" he speaks of the "ground of being." This "ground of being" is down for Tillich, not in the sense of down being inferior in some way but is the sense of metaphor. It is a different place, but a solid place (if I should be so bold as to say that). Based in the depth of the universe, it is rich and diverse. From the "creative ground" comes form and elements. Certainly, this is not all that far from Rogers's (1961) discussion on the "formative tendency," "actualization tendency," and "self-actualization."

Tillich agreed that what he described as "creative ground" and its depth has an impact of "person-to-person" encounters. The jargon was simply different in that Rogers used the phrase "forces in the universe."

In addressing what I called "awe," Tillich recalled something related Thomas Aquinas' theology: "If you know something, then you know something about God" (p. 75).

I experienced both Tillich and Rogers being in awe.

Rogers next sought to explore a different issue. What follows is a succinct and congruent presentation of Rogers's (1951) understanding of the process of therapy. It is also consistent with Rogers (1961) view of the "fully functioning person." He described the process as an issue of "what constitutes the optimal person" (p. 75). In this process, the person 1) moves towards "greater openness to experience;" 2) is "more able to listen to what's going on within himself;" 3) is "more sensitive to the reactions he's having to a given situation;" 4) is "more accurately perceptive of the world around him;" 5) is "realistic about what is going on within himself, as well as realistic about the world;" and 6) becomes "more social."

Tillich responded with two points. He called one "the way." He called the other "the aim." He related that he felt "familiar" with the issue of "openness." In this, he saw symbols functioning as a means of opening-up reality and something of oneself. He used word "soul" as being in relationship to this inner self. However, in this he said, "if this word were not forbidden in the university, I would call it something in our soul, but you know as a psychologist, as somebody who deals with the soul, that the word 'soul' is forbidden in academic contexts" (p. 76).

I experienced concern on hearing this. Tillich just used the word "soul" before a sophisticated assembly. That he perceived that the word was "forbidden" spoke loudly to me. The man saw atrocity in Nazi Germany, yet he was hesitant to use a religious word in America. Was there a glimpse here of oppression, not just irrelevancy of religion but a deliberate thwarting of religion by forbidding certain jargon?

Still, he used the word "soul." There did not appear to be any consequences for his use of the word. However, he still spoke of the taboo.

He reflected briefly on experiencing God or getting to "the divine spirit," saying that one does so by keeping oneself open. "You cannot force God down, you cannot produce the Divine Spirit in yourselves, but what you can do is open yourselves, to keep yourselves open to it" (p. 76).

Tillich stated that he agreed with Rogers about openness.

I doubted it. The two are coming from different places. Openness for Rogers is openness to self, and society. He did not speak about being open to discovering God. Rogers was thinking of the secular. Tillich though was coming from the sacred, or the spiritual. He was coming from another direction. Being open to oneself for Tillich, potentially, is being open to discovering God or the Divine Spirit. For Rogers, openness is self-discovery. For Tillich, one can discover God by being open.

Regarding "the aim," Tillich indicated it is 1) "realization of our true self;" 2) "bringing into actuality what is essentially given to us;" 3) "To become the way in which God sees us, in all our potentialities;" and 4) "to become more social."

For Tillich, this related to "agape." A person while trying to overcome "existential separation" finds acceptance by another. Tillich associated this not simply with human behavior. He associated it with "faith," "ultimate meaning of life," in relationship to the "ultimate aim of life." Again, Tillich's understanding of this is theological, not psychological. He did see in this an "affirming" of the other person, and oneself. "I wouldn't use the term 'self-love' — that's too difficult — but self-affirmation and self-acceptance, one of the most difficult things to reach" (p. 77).

My Closing Remarks

I did not find it easy to address the theology and the differences between Tillich and Rogers. I missed common ground here between Tillich and Rogers. I felt both men were getting at speaking to similar issues on estrangement/incongruence, acceptance, and openness. That one pointed to human beings as the end, and the other to discovering God as the end somehow almost did not matter. It might have been two ships passing in the night, not being on the same path and going in different directions. They shared fame, reputation, and a place in time.

Rogers noticed the themes of faith and love, but highlighted the person liking oneself. He associated this as a self-affirmation "in a healthy and useful fashion."

Rogers also pushed further on being "open to experience." This open person is constantly in a "valuing process." There is a valuing of "each moment" and of one's "behavior in each moment." The focus is on the person's self-actualization process and relates to the "mature person." Rogers also indicated a preference or believe that legalistic (my term) values from the past are probably not "appropriate or meaningful" as in the past. Like the issue of contemporary humankind's alleged movement away from religion or its irrelevancy, I have doubt that legalism has subsided. In fact, the contemporary persons of the times struggle with this as can easily be seen in news and media reports.

I found some danger in holding Rogers's statement too literally. There remains value in not stealing, cheating on one's spouse, or killing the convenient store clerk, or beating one's dog. How far Rogers's statement goes remains a matter of debate. I have had colleagues at conferences say that they thought it was OK to have sex with clients, while even the American Psychological Association considers such behavior unethical. The fact of the matter is that there is debate over what behaviors are valued. What is valued is not completely in the hands of any given person. A variety of perspectives and ideologies that come into play. Some prevail over others.

Tillich reacted in support of values asserting that he himself was "an outspoken critic of the philosophy of values." I suspect both men were referring to rigid legalism, which is mean spirited and disrespectful. Tillich believed that "agape, or love" should replace overbearing values. This love and listening go together. The listening leads to decisions for "action" and inner "satisfaction." In this, there can be "joy."

Rogers affirmed the listening stating it is about listening from within, to oneself, and for the other person.

This triggered my own position on empathy influenced greatly by the person-centered approach. The basic concept is that of entering the world of another as if . . .. The "as if" part is too broad to explore here. However, (Bower, 1985) held that one of the ways the therapist has a deeper understanding of the client is when the therapist experiences the same kinds of feelings that the client experiences. For instance, anger, hope, joy, sadness, etc. The therapist does not act out these feelings, though he or she might express them within the ethical guidelines of the profession. There is some legalism here. The therapist cannot go around doing whatever he or she wants to do because of his/her feelings in association with the client. Rather, I speak of using the feelings as a barometer or indicator of what the client is experiencing.

I find this informative not destructive. It becomes destructive when the therapist violates the principles of the person-centered approach. The alternative is to remain aloof and distant in the name of being objective and thus losing a valuable sense of knowing that comes with experiencing.

Tillich captured something that I feel is related to the position I just stated. "When I say listening to the situation, I mean the situation is constituted out of everything around me and myself, so listening love is always listening to both sides" (p. 78). I add that when I listen to me, I can also listen to the client. If I am detached from the client, and only listen to me, then I miss the client. I need to allow the client to affect me as I enter the client's world. When that happens, provided I am not defensive, frightened, disrespectful, or lose control of myself, I can learn something about the client.

Rogers revisited the infant's experience of fully experiencing one's self in context of others. "I feel that the small infant is a good example of the valuing process that is going on continuously. He isn't troubled by the concepts and standards that have been built up by adults, and he's continually valuing his experience as either making for his enhancement or being opposed to that actualization" (p. 78).

That is true at the cognitive level. However, the person-centered approach has placed a great deal of emphasis on being nonjudgmental. If I stick to the infant as a "good example," I have not met an infant yet that was not judgmental as hell. When an infant is crying, whether hunger, or a dirty diaper triggers the cry, that is a statement of "I don't like this!!!!!" Fix it!

I have met infants that experienced what they experienced in spite of the intellectual judgmentalness of the adults in their lives. Therefore, infants can have feelings, which run contrary to the feelings of their caregivers. Infants experience what they experience. As we grow older, we may all wish we had more access the part that makes our needs clear or expresses experiences without suppressing others.

Tillich said (and this astounded me as I have been writing this as I have read the material), "Now, this valuation, of course, would be not an intellectual valuation, but an evaluation with his whole being" (p. 78).

Rogers responded by saying, "I think of it as an organismic valuing process" (p. 78).

Finally, I share these final words from Tillich. Both men have an approach for wholeness, genuineness, completeness. The infant illustrated that completeness. They moved me not because of content. They were the last words he spoke at a public forum. "That means a reaction of his whole being, and I certainly believe that it is an adequate description" (p. 78).

References

Borg, M. J. (2001). *Reading the Bible again for the first time: Taking the Bible seriously but not literally.* New York: HarperCollins Publisher.

Bower, D. W. (1985). *Assumptions and attitudes of the Rogerian person-centered approach to counseling: Implications for pastoral counseling.* Unpublished Research Project, Columbia Theological Seminary, Decatur, GA.

Bozarth, J. (1998). *Person-centered therapy: A revolutionary paradigm.* Ross-on-Wye: PCCS Books.

Dawkins, R. (2006). *The God delusion.* New York: Houghton Mifflin.

D'Souza, D. (2007). *What's so great about Christianity.* Washington, D.C.: Regnery Publishing.

Fant, C. E., & Pinson Jr, W. (1971). *20 Centuries of Great Preaching: An Encyclopedia of Preaching,* 13 Volumes. Waco: Word Books.

Harris, S. (2004). The *end of faith: Religion, terror, and the future of reason.* New York: W. W. Norton

Hitchens, C. (2007). *God is not great: How religion poisons everything.* New York: Hachette Book Group.

Kirschenbaum, H. (1979). *On Becoming Carl Rogers.* New York, New York: Dell Publishing Co.

Kirschenbaum, H., & Henderson, V. L. (1989). *Carl Rogers dialogues.* Boston: Houghton Mifflin.

Rogers, C. R. (1939). *The clinical treatment of the problem child.* Boston: Houghton Mifflin.

Rogers, C. R. (1942). *Counseling and psychotherapy; newer concepts in practice.* Boston: Houghton Mifflin.

Rogers, C. R. (1951). *Client-centered therapy.* Boston: Houghton Mifflin.

Rogers, C. R. (1961). *On becoming a person.* Boston: Houghton Mifflin.

Rogers, C. R. (1986). Rogers, Kohut, and Erickson: A personal perspective and some similarities and difference. *Person-Centered Review*, 1(2), 125-140.

Spong, J. S. (2001). *A new Christianity for a new world: Why traditional faith is dying and how a new faith is being born.* New York: HarperCollins.

Tillich, P. (1955). *The new being.* New York: Charles Scribner's Sons.

The Paul Tillich - Carl Rogers Dialogue:

A Personal Annotation

(Part A)

While preparing a presentation for the Theological Study group of the Athens-Elberton District of the North Georgia Conference of the United Methodist Church, I decided to see if I could find a video of the Carl Rogers - Paul Tillich dialogue of 1965. I had the verbatim in Kirschenbaum and Henderson (1989). I even had an audio tape with a missing segment. I have since misplaced that tape during cleaning out old stuff experiences. A video is presently available on Youtube. Given how the Internet resources change quickly.

I have already presented the verbatim in an earlier chapter, including the ah-s and um-s. My twist to that in this chapter is to annotate the verbatim with my observations. They reflect my views as a person who has held an orthodox view of Christianity as a United Methodist. I also studied Tillich's three volume systematic theology with Ben Kline at Columbia Theological Seminary, which is a Presbyterian USA seminary in Decatur, Ga. Allegedly, Dr. Kline was regarded as an expert on Tillich. I have not had occasion this side of my studies to see his name formally associated with any articles or books. That doesn't matter because my experience with him was quite positive. However, I hardly became an expert myself and struggle to understand Paul Tillich.

On the other hand, I have had occasion to work with the Person-Centered Approach for many years. I have a few articles and a couple of insignificant books on the approach. Until a few years ago, I was active in a small but international network of people who espoused the approach.

Regarding this dialogue, the recording appears to me to begin a little after the start of the interaction. I believe that material I heard but now can no longer find may have been a part of the material no longer available on any well-known recordings of the Tillich-Rogers dialogue. The opening of the verbatim seems to miss the basis for Rogers' opening remark.

The annotations must be viewed as mine. That is, I make no pretense to think I can speak to Rogers or Tillich. I have no pretense of being an expert. I make no pretense to be an accurate exegetical commentary of what Rogers or Tillich mean by their comments. I can only share my perspectives and do so to the best of my ability. I also make no pretense to claim I liked what the two said. Even if my own response is awkward in comparison to these two giants in their fields, I have shared my views. I do hold the pretense that awkward or not, they genuinely reflect my observations and stances including my traditional Methodist position.

The Presentation

When I made the presentation, I had a video to show. During presentation we stopped to talk, and communication broke down between the computer and the projector. I had no clue how to correct that and fearful that it would take too much time, I defaulted to the verbatim. Doing so missed a great deal as it deprived us of seeing Rogers and Tillich (especially his rich German accent) interacting and engaging with each other.

Dialogue with Annotation

CARL ROGERS: *The importance of self-affirmation: I think that would be one area where we agree.*

Rogers placed a great deal of emphasis on valuing persons. So much so that, in the classic (1957) position on the necessary and sufficient conditions for therapeutic change, he asserted that there is a need for unconditional positive regard. Further, he was well known for speaking about the positive foundation of every human being. "Seeing the human organism has essentially positive in nature - is profoundly radical flies in the face of traditional psychoanalysis, runs counter to the Christian tradition, as opposed to the philosophy of most institutions, including our educational institutions. In psychoanalytic theory hard-core is seen as untamed, wild, constructive. Christian theology we are "conceived in sin," and evil by nature. In our institution the individual is seen as untrustworthy. Persons must be guided, corrected, disciplined, punished, so that they will not follow the pathway set by their nature." (Rogers, 1986, p. 127). Rogers position on this runs counter to Tillich as well. Thus, the agreement cannot be about humans being basically good. If there is agreement it would be based on a need for self-affirmation given the circumstances of life. For Tillich those circumstances include being alienated and estranged from God and from one another.

CARL ROGERS: *Then I have been much impressed with your thinking about the courage to be, because I see that in psychotherapy; the courage of being something, the risk that is involved in knowing. . . .*

Rogers spoke on becoming a person. Tillich spoke of courage to be this way. "The use of the term 'courage' in this context (fully explained in my book The Courage to Be) needs some interpretation, especially in its relation to faith. In a short formulation one could say that courage is that element in faith which is related to the risk of faith. One cannot replace faith by courage, but neither can one describe faith without courage" (Tillich, 2011, p. 127). Tillich (2008) did connect courage to be and self-affirmation. "Both the doctrines about man and the help given to man are a matter of cooperation from many points of view. Only in this way is it possible to understand and to actualize man's power of being, his essential self-affirmation, his courage to be" (Kindle Locations 1132-1134).

CARL ROGERS: *I've also liked your phrase about him the antimoral act being one that contradicts the realization of the individual, and it seems to me both of us are trying to push beyond some of the trends that are very prominent in the modern world; the logical positivistic, the ultrascientific approach, the stress of the mechanistic and highly deterministic point of view which, as I see it, makes man just an object trying to find some alternative stance in relation to life. I wonder if you feel that we're in some agreement on issues of that sort?*

When I think "antimoral" I think permissiveness to do whatever one wants. Trends in our time have related to sexual permissiveness, the use of recreational drugs, divorce, and other behaviors. My interpretation is out of sync with what the concept means. Rogers is pointing to dehumanization of human beings. He wrote (1977), "politics, and present-day psychological and social usage, has to do with power and control: the extent to which persons desire attempt to obtain, possess, share, or surrender power and control over others and/or themselves. It has to do with the maneuvers, the strategies and tactics, witting or unwitting, by which such power and control over one's own life and others' lives is sought and gained--or shared or relinquished. It has to do with the *locus of decision-making power*: who makes the decisions which, consciously or unconsciously, regulate or control the thoughts, feelings, and behavior of others or oneself . . ." (p. 4).

For Rogers this misuse of this and the imposing of power is at the heart of dehumanization and enables behaviors that have adverse impacts on persons and society.

PAUL TILLICH: *Yes, of course. In all these points I heartily agree, and I am very glad you enumerate them for me.*

CARL ROGERS: *Well, perhaps we could push into some areas where I am not quite so sure. I wonder what some of your views are about the nature of man. When I've been asked about that - I think some of the existentialists take the point of view that man really has no nature, but it seems to me that he has - I have taken the point of view that man belongs to a particular species. He has species characteristics. One of those, I think, being the fact that he is incurably social; I think he has a deep need for relationships. Then I think that simply because man is an organism he tends to be directional. He's moving in the direction of actualizing himself. So, for myself, I really feel man does have a describable nature. I have been interested, for example, in the I fact that you discuss the demonic aspects of man. I don't know whether you see that as a part of his nature - at any rate I would be interested in your views in regard to the nature of man.*

What I heard concerning the nature of man:

1) Existentialists say man has no nature.
2) Rogers believes man does have a nature.
   a) Belongs to a species (oddly I see that as a form of dehumanization since we use the term species to categorize non-human living entities).
   b) Human beings are social and are thus in need of relationships.
   c) Is an organism (Further dehumanization through intellectualizing?)
   d) Human beings tend to be directional (at the heart of this is the actualizing tendency and its relative

self-actualization. ("Man's tendency to actualize himself, to become his potentialities. By this I mean the directional trend is evident in all organic life – encouraged to expand, expand, develop, mature – tendency to express and activate all the capacities of the organism, or the self" (Rogers 1961, p. 351)).

e) This nature is describable.

f) Rogers was interested in Tillich's stance on "demonic aspects of man." (I keep in mind Rogers makes this statement in the context of his positive view of human nature).

PAUL TILLICH: *Your question is very far-reaching and demands of me a little bit longer answer. The first point I want to make is that man, definitively, has a nature, and I think the best way to prove this is negatively, by showing how impossible the argument is if somebody denies that man has a nature.*

If Tillich is an existentialist, he basically just offered precision to the generalization that Rogers made that existentialists don't believe man has a nature. That is, he sharpened it by pointing to the opposite. In this case, addressing denying a nature of man.

PAUL TILLICH: *I think of the famous French existentialist, Sartre, who has denied that man has a nature and has emphasized that man is everything he makes of himself and this is his freedom.*

This seemed like both an affirmation about the issue of man not having a nature while also an affirmation that there is a nature, in this case what "man makes of himself" and the "freedom" associated with it. As an observer I cannot in this statement say what it means for one to make one's self according to Tillich's interpretation of Sartre, nor could I do that with "freedom."

PAUL TILLICH: *But, if he says that this is man's freedom to make himself, then this, of course, means that he has the nature of freedom, which other species do not have. To make such statements is somehow self-contradictory.*

Tillich takes note of a contradiction. I do not have specifics about what this means.

PAUL TILLICH: *Even if you attribute to man what medieval theology attributed to God, namely to be by himself, and not conditioned by anything else, even then you cannot escape the statement that man has a nature. Now that's my answer to the first element in your question, but there are two more and I want to get at them.*

It would appear to me that Tillich is saying there is a nature and no way to say that man has no nature. We have no description here of that nature. He speaks of medieval theology in this and thus has presuppositions of that.

There also appears to me something of sovereignty and radical uniqueness of God in Tillich's statement. God is what God is and has a nature. Man is what man is, and even using medieval theology (for which I am unclear what Tillich had in mind constitutes medieval theology), man has a nature. I am lacking in what those descriptions are. I suspect in part that medieval theology is man was created in the image of God and even as a Fallen creature the Divine spark remains, even in the corruption of having fell.

PAUL TILLICH: *The second is that I distinguish, so to speak, two natures of man. or one which one rightly calls his nature and the other which is a mixture of accepting and distorting his true nature.*

There is some apparent separation here as, again Rogers, holds that man is basically good. However, Rogers also speaks about incongruence. This incongruence though is not the foundational nature of man, rather congruence is. We are essentially broken in relationship to the absence or low quality of relationships around us. A way to describe this in part would be like this: "There is a considerable degree of incongruence between the sensory and visceral experience of the organism, and the structure of the self, the former involving much that is denied to awareness, and the latter involving an awareness of much that is not so" (p. 529).

Tillich doesn't necessarily assert man is basically good, but the true nature is distorted thus virtually divided in nature. The focus with Tillich is to acknowledge and grasp that the human being is estranged (Tillich, 1951) Taking such a stance essentially does say that man's true nature might be basically good, but in our estrangement anxiety and meaninglessness blocks awareness of that goodness. In a Preface regarding Victor Frankl's (1963) work, Gordon Allport offered a statement that probably captures Tillich's position well. An existential theme is "to live is to suffer, to survive is to find meaning in the suffering. If there is a purpose to life at all, there must be a purpose in suffering and in dying. But no man can tell another what this purpose is. Each must find out for himself and must accept the responsibility that his answer prescribes. If he succeeds, he will continue to grow in spite of all indignities" (xi).

A Lutheran position, under which Tillich was raised, would be hard pressed to deny that man is not also basically good with man being created by God. However, it would strongly speak to the sinful condition of man. The sinful condition runs counter to Rogers' more optimistic position. Rogers asserted that by creating a positive environment the creative resourceful person could emerge. Tillich asserted that accessing the anxiety of the person opened to door to a new being. The more ancient position is not seen so compatible in the modern world as it was in former times. Tillich has essentially remythologized theological jargon. I am convinced Rogers also remythologized as well.

PAUL TILLICH: *The first one I would call, with a very vague term, his true nature, but to make it less vague I usually call it his essential nature. If I speak theologically, then I call it man's created nature, and you remember that this is one of the main points about which the early church was tremendously fighting — namely, that man's essential or created nature is good. According to the biblical word, "God looked at everything he had created and behold! it was very good." There is an even more philosophical, reformulated affirmation of this by Augustine, namely, Esse qua esse bonum est, which means in English, "being as being is good."*

Following my claim that Tillich didn't necessarily assert man is good, he does though point out that at creation, (keeping in mind that Tillich is far from a literalist concerning the Genesis account), all that was made was declared by God to be "very good." In a sense, this does not matter at the same time there exists another nature.

PAUL TILLICH: *Now that is what I would call man's essential nature and then, from this, we must distinguish man's existential nature, of which I would say it has a characteristic of being estranged from his true nature. Man, as he is in time and space, in biography and history, this man is not simply the opposite of man's essential nature, for then it wouldn't be man any longer. But his temporal, historical nature is a distortion of his essential nature, and in attempting to reach it, he may be contradicting his true nature. It is a tremendous mixture, and in order to understand the real human predicament, we must distinguish these two elements. I believe that in Freud, himself, and much Freudianism and psychotherapy generally, there is no clear distinction of these two points. This was your second element.*

There is an important contrast here. Rogers, while speaking about incongruence, does not and was not willing to go this far with incongruence. Tillich asserts that in the existential nature, man is "estranged" from his true nature. The true nature is distorted. It is so distorted that it cannot be accessed and thus cannot be described or experienced.

Personally, I am willing to acknowledge that. Rogers honed in on the notion that man was basically good. Tillich speaks more profoundly to estrangement being a radical brokenness or alienation from the true nature. Rogers indicates the goodness of man can be tapped by providing certain attitudinal qualities (empathy, acceptance, and genuineness). Tillich though sees the distortion even in the qualities. They are limited because of man's estrangement from the true self.

On one hand, Tillich may appear to be more in sync with the human condition than Rogers if we consider that in the 70+ years that Rogers' theory has impacted counseling and psychotherapy, there is no indication the world is a better behaving world.

However, on the other hand, Rogers has shown that providing an environment rich in empathy, acceptance, and genuineness does foster constructive creative change in individuals and with some institutional models. It does facilitate change in the broken world. There just isn't enough of it. One doesn't have to deliberately engage one's angst and anxiety.

PAUL TILLICH: *Now shall I answer your third element also . . . ?*

CARL ROGERS: *First . . . let me make one comment on this. I find in my work as a therapist that if I can create a climate of the utmost of freedom for the other individual, I can really trust the directions that he will move. That is, people sometimes say l to me "What if you create a climate of freedom? A man might use this freedom to become completely evil or antisocial." I don't find that to be true, and this is one of the things that makes me feel that – I don't know whether this is essentially or existentially – in a relationship of real freedom the individual tends to move not only toward deeper self-understanding, but toward more social behavior.*

These two were not speaking in the same arena. Rogers is speaking about psychology or human behavior. Tillich, a theologian, is speaking about ontology and the human condition which impacts psychology. There is no indication that the human conditions of empathy, acceptance, and genuineness are more pronounced in our time than any other time in history. In fact, brokenness remains even if it has become more pronounced in spite of the work of Rogers and colleagues. Empathy, acceptance and genuineness are behaviors are basic to man. So is misunderstanding, rejection, and the propensity to put up facades.

That being said, from an anecdotal stance, there have been many stories of change and renewal via the use of the person-centered approach. Further, research has borne out the success of the person-centered approach to therapy (Bozarth, 1998).

The concern addressed by Rogers that people will move in negative directions in their freedom holds more firmly in the absence of the conditions of empathy, acceptance, and genuineness than in environments rich in these conditions. Many of us have seen data asserting that our prisons are full of people from broken homes and environments.

PAUL TILLICH: Yes, now I would put a question mark to this, and I would say that first of all, who is free enough to create this situation of freedom for the others?

There is further contrast here. Rogers concept of freedom might be somewhat qualified with offering certain conditions, but Rogers espouses constructive choices in the presence of the conditions.

PAUL TILLICH: And since I call this mixture of man's essential nature and his estranged nature ambiguous – the realm of the ambiguity of life – I would say under the condition of this ambiguity, nobody is able to create this sphere of freedom.

Tillich though is wondering if freedom is possible at all since man's nature is distorted.

PAUL TILLICH: But now let's suppose that it exists in some other way. I can come to this later when we speak of the demonic. Then I still would say the individual who lives in such a social group in which freedom is given to him remains an ambiguous mixture between essential and existential being. He is, as the English language expresses it beautifully, "in a predicament, and this predicament is a universal, tragic estrangement from one's true being. Therefore, I don't believe in the power of the individual to use his freedom in the way in which he should – namely, fulfilling one's own essential potentialities, or essentialities; these two words are here the same. So, I am more skeptical, both about the creation of such a situation and about the individuals who are in such a situation.

This further illustrates the contrast. Can the existential nature fix itself? The fix is ultimate concern – faith (Tillich 2011). There is qualification with Tillich regarding this faith: "Another example— almost a counter-example, yet nevertheless quality revealing— is the ultimate concern with "success" and with social standing and economic power. It is the god of many people in the highly competitive Western culture and it does what every ultimate concern must do: it demands unconditional surrender to its laws even if the price is the sacrifice of genuine human relations, personal conviction, and creative eros. Its threat is social and economic defeat, and its promise— indefinite as all such promises— the fulfillment of one's being. It is the breakdown of this kind of faith which characterizes and makes religiously important most contemporary literature. Not false calculations but a misplaced faith is revealed in novels like Point of No Return. When fulfilled, the promise of this faith proves to be empty" (pp. 3-4).

-I have no reason to think Tillich could not also use the terms psychology or education in this "counter-example."

CARL *ROGERS: I would agree on the difficulty of creating complete freedom. I am sure none of us is ever able to really create that for another person in its completeness. . . . Yet what impresses me is that even imperfect attempts to create a climate of freedom and acceptance and understanding seem to liberate the person to move toward really social goals. I wonder if it is your thinking about the demonic aspect that makes you put a question mark after that.*

Rogers wrote a great deal of material and I have a limited ability to remember. I have no recollection of Rogers speaking about the limits of freedom. It makes some sense that Rogers would acknowledge this considering he asserts that there are necessary and sufficient conditions in regards for facilitating therapeutic change. His material on "A Way of Being" pushes those conditions into the world in general. My own work "Person-Centered/Client-Centered: Applications for Living (2000) was based on living out the conditions in a variety of settings.

Rogers in this limitation of freedom sought to facilitate change. He wrote, "I am hypothesizing that significant positive personality change does not occur except in a relationship" (Rogers, 1989, p. 221).

PAUL *TILLICH: Now, let me first answer you about what you just said, and here I would very much agree. I would say there are fragmentary actualizations in history and 1 agree especially with the deep insight we have gained, largely by psychotherapy, about the tremendous importance of love in earliest ages of the development of children.*

Tillich is limited to a psychoanalytic framework which Rogers was exposed to in his career but abandoned.

PAUL *TILLICH: So, the question would come here: "Where are the forces which create a situation in which the child receives that love which gives him, later on, the freedom to face life and not to escape from life into neuroses and psychoses?" I leave that question open.*

Indeed, the open question is addressed by uncounted theorists including Freud, Beck, Erickson, Maslow and Rogers.

"If children live with criticism, they learn to condemn.

If children live with hostility, they learn to fight.

If children live with fear, they learn to be apprehensive.

If children live with pity, they learn to feel sorry for themselves.

If children live with ridicule, they learn to feel shy.

If children live with jealousy, they learn to feel envy.

If children live with shame, they learn to feel guilty.

If children live with encouragement, they learn confidence.

If children live with tolerance, they learn patience.

If children live with praise, they learn appreciation.

If children live with acceptance, they learn to love.

If children live with approval, they learn to like themselves . . . ." (Nolte, 1972)

Whether positive or negative, there are intangible realities that impact choice and thus freedom.

PAUL *TILLICH: But now you are interested about the demonic, and you are not the only one. I myself was, and everybody is in some way, so let me say how I came to this concept. I wrote in the year 1926', when 1 was still professor at the University of Dresden Germany, a little article, a little pamphlet, The Demonic, and the reason not to speak of*

the "fallen" or the "sinful men" or any of these phrases was that I saw
from two points of view structures which are stronger than the good will
of the individual, and one of these structures was the neurotic-psychotic
structure. I came into contact after the First World War, since 1920
about, with the psychoanalytic movement, coming from Freud at that
time, and changing the climate of the whole century – already in Europe
at the time.

Tillich developed his grounds for the Demonic and it, as well, points to the problem of restriction on freedom. I personally note that he refers to the 'fallen' and the 'sinful men' as he does so. It appears to me to be sort of a demythologizing of the concepts. I have no confidence that Tillich would have acknowledged this statement I just made. He used traditional words in dealing with the Demonic but indicated the Demonic while not speaking in those traditional words. I am though hard pressed to say not using the traditional terms does not speak to them. The jargon is simply different.

Tillich is though highlighting very quickly aspects in the human condition that "are stronger than the good will of the individual." Freedom thus is limited by these.

PAUL TILLICH: The second was the analysis of the conflicts of
society by the Socialist movement and especially by the early writings of
Karl Marx, and in both cases, I found a phenomenon for which these
traditional terms, like "fallen men" and "sinful men," are not sufficient.
The only sufficient term I found was in the New Testament use of the
term "demonic," which is in the stories about Jesus: similar to being
possessed.

From a subjective standpoint, despite Tillich's reputation and intelligence, is the word "demonic" really more sufficient than the traditional terms "'fallen men' and 'sinful men'"?

PAUL TILLICH: That means a force, under a force, which is
stronger than the individual good will. And so I used that term. Of
course, I emphasized very much I don't mean it in a mythological sense –
as little demons or a personal Satan running around the world – but
I mean it as structures which are ambiguous, both to a certain extent

creative, but ultimately destructive. This is the reason why I introduced that term. So, instead of only speaking of estranged mankind, and not using the old terminology anyhow, I had to find a term which covers the transpersonal power which takes hold of men and of society; of men in stages, let's say, of drunkenness, being a drunkard, and not being able to overcome it, or producing a society in which either class conflicts or as today in the whole world, conflicts of great ideologies, of great forms of political faiths which struggle with each other – and every step to overcome them has usually the consequence of driving the people more deeply into them Now this is what I meant with the demonic. So, I hope I made one thing clear: that I don't mean it in the old mythological sense which of course has to be demythologized.

Tillich's description here really isn't all that far from the description of sin by Calvin, Luther, or others. The terms used may be more contemporary and even Tillich's term "demonic" is not generally used in our time. The term carries with it a sense of being possessed. However, the main thrust of Tillich's position is destructive and perhaps self-destructive nature of humankind.

CARL ROGERS: . . . And certainly, when I look at some of the things going on in the world from the power point of view and so on, I can see why you might think in terms of demonic structures.

While Rogers has an optimistic view of human behavior under the circumstances of the necessary and sufficient conditions, and probably in terms of the many times human beings have overcome terrible atrocities, he is not in denial of atrocities. "I would not want to be misunderstood on this. I do not have a Pollyanna view of human nature. I am quite aware that how of defensiveness interfere individuals can do behave in ways which are incredibly cruel, or destructive, immature, regressive, anti–social, hurtful. Yet one of the most refreshing and invigorating parts of my experience is to work with such individuals and to discover the strongly positive correctional tendencies which exist in, as in all of this, at the deepest levels" (Rogers, 1961, p. 27).

CARL ROGERS: I'd like to talk a little bit about the way I see this matter of alienation and estrangement. It seems to me that the infant is not estranged from himself. To me it seems that the infant is a whole and integrated organism, gradually individual, and that the estrangement that occurs is one that he learns — that in order to preserve the love of others, parents usually, he takes into himself as something he has experienced for himself, the judgments of his parents: just like the small boy who has been rebuked for pulling his sister's hair goes around saying, "bad boy, bad boy." Meanwhile, he is pulling her hair again. In other words, he has introjected the notion that he is bad, where actually he is enjoying the experience, and it is this estrangement between what he is experiencing and the concepts he links up with what he is experiencing that seems to me to constitute the basic estrangement. I don't know whether you want to comment on that . . .

I part company myself from Rogers regarding the estrangement issue. Up until birth, the infant has been in a warm, dark world. We assume it is a safe environment, with low stress. In fact, death occurs there. Assuming it is safe and warm, the infant is suddenly thrown into a bright world. At the time of Rogers and Tillich many received a slap on the fanny in welcome. Allegedly it was designed to trigger breathing in this world. The infant is thrust into estrangement from the only environment it has known. Surely that represents alienation well and estrangement. It has no idea if it is really welcome or if it will be met with adversity right away. It has suddenly experienced bright lights, colder temperatures, and touches, that slap had to be painful as well as the bright lights and new noises.

Granted, the baby carries no presuppositions, thus it cries and/or coos. It sleeps, sees, hears, tastes, feels, and responds and reacts. The reactions seem oft times to be appropriate. Other times the reactions puzzle and overwhelm adults. I can remember being unable to calm my daughters at times not knowing why they were in distress. Persistence helped, but often it seemed that they changed their behaviors despite my efforts and the efforts of others to help them. Then suddenly they became comfortable.

As they got older they found ways to be less uncontrolled of themselves ("uncontrolled" may not even be a good word. They might have been very controlled and controlling).

All this and more contributes to my suspecting they were estranged from their own personal ability to calm themselves.

However, a baby crying is a baby crying. A baby laughing is a baby laughing. It is what it is and there are no "you ought not" thoughts flowing through their minds. They learn "oughts." They then may become estranged from their own feelings because of the lessons they learn from the older people in their lives.

Rogers' positive view comes through here even if it is just a glimpse.

PAUL *TILLICH: Yes; because the infant is a very important problem; I call this in philosophical or, better, psychological terms, the mythological state of Adam and Eve before the Fall: dreaming innocence. It has not yet reached reality; it is still dreaming. Of course, this also is a symbol, but it is a symbol which is nearer to our psychological language than the Fall of Adam and Eve, but it means the same thing, and it means that Adam, namely men - the Hebrew "Adam" means men — that men, every man, is in the process of transition from dreaming innocence to conscious self-actualization, and in this process the estrangement also takes place, as well as the fulfillment; therefore, my concept of ambiguity. I agree with you that there is also in what the parents used to call "bad boy" or "bad girl," there is also a necessary act of self-fulfillment, but there is also something asocial in it, because it hurts his sister and so it has to be repressed, and whether we say "bad boy," or prevent it in any other way, this is equally necessary, and these experiences mean for me the slow process of transition from dreaming innocence into self-actualization on the one side and self-estrangement on the other side, and these two acts are ambiguously intermixed. Now that would be about my interpretation of the situation of the infants.*

There is distraction in our scientific age in dealing with the Biblical Adam and Eve. A handful of people including me take the creation epic quite seriously. However, it cannot be denied it does not fit well with contemporary positions on the beginnings of things. Even the Big Bang, which allegedly occurred suddenly, runs counter to the creation description of Genesis.

Thus, it is hard to speak to Adam & Eve as estrangement and distortion of human nature.

What can we get from the story in this context? There is support for Tillich's position on estrangement. Here he uses the story to illustrate the human condition. I am quite convinced that even as Tillich uses contemporary language and may have even believed his position was universal, he is consistent with the Lutheran position and probably the Reformed tradition as well on this issue. Even taking out Adam and Eve from the equation, the reality is the people feel estranged, if not from God, from themselves and others. Even the late pop singer Sammy Davis Jr. used the words, "I've got to be me" in one of the songs he sang, and his peer the late Frank Sinatra sang, "I did it my way." Both songs reflect that struggle to be one's self, if not directly, indirectly by highlighting the phrases.

In a more realistic way, the problem of being a child and parenting and the growing up process whereby the infant encounters both encouraging and discouraging statements. In this case, "bad boy"/ "bad girl" remarks.

With Rogers these labels run counter to the child's real experience as natural impulses or behaviors are judged and labeled as "bad." To the child they are what they are, experiences and behaviors. Rogers holds this contributes to becoming incongruent.

I differ from Rogers; I think babies are perfectly capable to declaring what is "bad" and they do so. They get more verbal and nonverbal feedback as they get older. This then contributes, as far as I am concerned, to incongruence, and thus suppression of experiences.

Tillich though has room for suppression of behaviors that hurt others. So, if the brother pulls his sister's hair and hurts her, a parent can and perhaps should deal directly with that. There is a need for clear "correction." This "correction" probably does facilitate incongruence. "I want to pull my sister's hair" gets channeled into something else because it has been discouraged and thus suppressed by the boy who is responding to external pressure.

CARL *ROGERS: Well, there is much in that that I would agree with.*

I had a hard time seeing how there was much in Tillich's statement that Rogers would agree with considering his nondirective stance. He hardly comes close to strong correction and repression of behavior in another of his writings (Rogers 1977). He further basically asserted that in being open to the directions and choices that a person, including a child, would make would help facilitation. "The individual in this nurturing climate is free to choose any direction, but actually selects positive and constructive ways (Rogers, 1980, p. 134).

CARL *ROGERS: I'd like to say a little bit about the kind of relationship in which I think man's estrangement can be healed, as I see it from my own experience. For example, when we talk about – when either of us talks about the courage to be or the tendency to become oneself, I feel that perhaps that can only be fully achieved in a relationship. Perhaps the best example of what I am talking about is that I believe that the person can only accept the unacceptable in himself when he is in a close relationship in which he experiences acceptance. This, I think, is a large share of what constitutes psychotherapy – that the individual finds that the feelings he has been ashamed of or that he has been unable to admit into his awareness, that those can be accepted by another person, so then he becomes able to accept them as a part of himself. I don't know too much of your thinking about interpersonal relationships, but I wonder how that sounds to you.*

My own inclination here is to consider Roger's position on incongruence. This can be described as essentially a disconnect between experience and awareness. For instance, the person may be experiencing sadness and unaware of it (Rogers, 1961). Incongruence can also be about not connecting with one's social world, the shy person, for instance, feeling out of place in a crowd and not knowing how to get connected. Rogers (1957) connects incongruence with vulnerability and anxiety.

This probably is not all that far away from Tillich's theological position on estrangement and alienation even as Tillich is dealing with faith and theology (1954, 1957). Tillich's position is not only about not being connected to the ultimate being, it is also about not being connected to the one who exists amid others who exist.

PAUL *TILLICH: I believe that you are absolutely right in saying that the man-to-man experience of forgiveness, or better, acceptance of the unacceptable, is a very necessary precondition for self-affirmation. And you cannot forgive yourself, you cannot accept yourself.*

The word "forgiveness" does not appear in Rogers' works (1951, 1961, 1980). If people are basically good, then forgiveness is not the issue. Thus, Tillich and Rogers differ here. Tillich has room for accepting the unacceptable who are estranged and broken.

Rogers believes everyone is acceptable, so offer the acceptance. If someone is unacceptable it is an issue of judgmentalness not brokenness. If there is brokenness it is because the acceptable has not been accepted and the consequences result in persons experiencing incongruence. This is dealt with using unconditional positive regard which is not the same as forgiveness.

Tillich's release is to take note of being unacceptable and letting it go through forgiveness which doesn't necessary remove being unacceptable. The person is still broken. Forgiveness is a release of consequences, or not delving out consequences by accepting the unacceptable.

PAUL *TILLICH: If you look in the spiritual mirror, then you are much more prone to hate yourself and to be disgusted with yourself. So I believe that all forms of confessional in the churches and the confessions between friends and married people – and now the sacro-analytic confession of one's deeper levels which are opened up by the analyst – that without these things, there is no possibility of experiencing something which belongs ultimately to another dimension: the dimension of the ultimate, let me call it preliminarily. But I would say, with you, only the right acceptance is the medium through which it is necessary men have to go - from men to men - before the dimension of the ultimate is possible. I may add here that I have not used often anymore the word "forgiveness," because this often produces a bad superiority in him who forgives and the humiliation of him who is forgiven.*

The Rogerian model in this is to move towards positive regard of one's self. Tillich's model is to engage the estranged, not the one who is good. Rogers wants to access the good that exists. Tillich finds estrangement is overcome by confronting the estrangement by forgiveness.

PAUL *TILLICH: Therefore, I prefer the concept of acceptance. If you accept this acceptance, then I think I can confess that I have learned it from psychoanalysis. I have learned to translate an ideological concept which doesn't communicate any longer and replaced it by the way in which the psychoanalyst accepts his patients: not judging him, not telling him first he should be good, otherwise I cannot accept you, but accepting him just because he is not good, but he has something within himself that wants to be good.*

Acceptance in the psychoanalytic model is not the same as acceptance in the humanistic model. In the psychoanalytic model I accept your brokenness and point it out via interpretation, diagnosis, and analysis. There are protocols for doing that (free association, and dream analysis being among the older methods). Interpretation by the master analysis is significant as the patient in his/her life's circumstances is too defensive to see the real problem.

Rogers did not have the same positive view of psychoanalytic acceptance and nonjudgmentalness that Tillich expressed here. In fact, Rogers denies that acceptance and nonjudgmentalness is a significant part of psychoanalysis.

The contemporary psychoanalytic practitioner is allegedly more empathic and thus accepting than the earlier school. However, there are many psychoanalytic and psychodynamic practitioners who assert they know better about what the client is experiencing and how the client should get well (if that is possible) than the client (Bozarth, 1998).

I recently had an interaction with a social worker regarding a Hepatitis C patient. As an intern fresh out of school and never having worked with the person we were addressing, and not having worked with Hepatitis C patients at all she decided a patient was not going to be able to make it through treatment. My own position is for the professionals involved not to make such assumptions and find ways to help the person make it through treatment.

In short Tillich's position and Rogers on the issue are not the same. Acceptance for Tillich is acceptance of estrangement with forgiveness at the heart of that acceptance. Acceptance for Rogers is the person is basically good with acceptance being unconditional positive regard of the person.

CARL *ROGERS: Certainly, in my own experience, the potency of acceptance of another person has been demonstrated time and time again, when an individual feels that he is both fully accepted in all that he has been able to express and yet prized as a person. This has a very potent influence on his life and on his behavior.*

At the heart of Rogers position is acceptance which he long associated with unconditional positive regard. "To the extent that the therapist finds himself experiencing a warm acceptance of each aspect of the client's experience as being a part of that client, he is experiencing unconditional positive regard" (Rogers, 1989, p. 225).

PAUL *TILLICH: Yes, now I believe that this is really the center of what we call the "good news" in the Christian message.*

After I have just spent some energy saying Tillich and Rogers haven't been speaking the same language, Tillich gives a brief indication that he agrees with Rogers.

But does he? Rogers does not use the term "good news." He makes no claim that his is a Christian message though he himself was raised in the Congregationalist tradition. (I have mistakenly identified this tradition as Calvinistic. It is of the broader Reformed Tradition with John Wycliffe being an influence among others in the Reformed movement). A mission trip to China changed his theology as did a brief stint at Union Seminary in New York (Kirschenbaum, 1979). After that, efforts to claim Rogers message is Christian are difficult to make. This may not be because of practice and the articulation of the person-centered approach, but because it became so connected to the Humanistic camp that adherents aren't very likely to affirm the Christian influences on Rogers. Kirschenbaum though deals with Rogers Christian background. One is hard pressed to say that Rogers was not influenced by that background.

However, Rogers was not offering overt theological "good news" as promoted by the wide range of traditional Christian theologies and interpretations of scripture and tradition. Tillich though is, even though Tillich (1957) offered a different jargon and thus different symbols regarding faith.

References

Bozarth, J. (1998). *Person-centered therapy: A revolutionary paradigm.* Ross-on-Wye: PCCS Books.

Frankl, V. E. (1963). Man's search for meaning: An introduction to logotherapy. New York, New York: Pocket Books.

Kirschenbaum, H. (1979). *On becoming Carl Rogers.* New York, New York: Dell Publishing.

Kirschenbaum, H., & Henderson, V. L. (1989). *Carl Rogers: Dialogues.* New York, New York: Dell Publishing.

Nolte, D. L. (1972). *Children learn what they live.* Retrieved from http://www.empowermentresources.com/info2/childrenlearn-long_version.html

Rogers (1951). *Client centered therapy.* Boston: Houghton Mifflin.

Rogers (1957). *The necessary and sufficient conditions of therapeutic personality change,* Journal of Consulting Psychology,21(2), 95-103.

Rogers, C. R. (1961). *On becoming a person*. Boston: Houghton Mifflin.

Rogers, C. R. (1977). *On personal power*. New York, New York: A Delta Book, Dell Publishing.

Rogers, C. R. (1980). *A way of being*. Boston: Houghton Mifflin.

Rogers, C. R. (1986). *Rogers. Kohut, and Erickson: A personal perspective on some similarities and differences*. The Person-Centered Review. Sage Publications, 1(2).

Rogers, C. R. (1989). *The necessary and sufficient conditions of therapeutic personality change*. In H, Kirschenbaum, & V. L. Henderson, (Eds.) The Carl Rogers reader. Boston: Houghton Mifflin, pp. 219-235.

Tillich, P. (1951). Systematic Theology, Vol. 1. Three volumes in one. Chicago: University of Chicago Press.

Tillich, P. (1954). *The courage to be*. New Haven: Yale University Press.

Tillich, P. (1957). Systematic Theology, Vol. 2. Three volumes in one. Chicago: University of Chicago Press.

Tillich, Paul (2008). *The courage to be* (The Terry Lectures Series) (Kindle Location 1220). Yale University Press. Kindle Edition.

Tillich, Paul (2011). *Dynamics of faith* (Perennial Classics) (p. 120). HarperCollins. Kindle Edition.

The Paul Tillich - Carl Rogers Dialogue:

A Personal Annotation

(Part B)

[Intermission.]

PAUL TILLICH: *The minister, who represents the ultimate meaning of life, can have much skill unconsciously, although he is unskilled, but even then he should not establish himself as a second-rate psychotherapist. Now that seems to me a very important rule. Otherwise, cooperation would soon end in little catastrophes and would come to an end altogether.*

Tillich's faith as ultimate concern is not the same as Rogers' actualization tendency. Ultimate concern is not the same as ultimate meaning in life but is part of it. Ultimate meaning might be part of self-actualization in as much as becoming a "fully functioning person" (Rogers, 1980) means experiencing the possibility of an openness to a faith realm, but it is not necessary to the world of the "fully functioning person" from a psycho-social perspective.

Ultimate Concern with an accompanying ultimate meaning is far more reaching for Tillich (1957). "Faith is the state of being ultimately concerned: the dynamics of faith are the dynamics of man's ultimate concern. Man, like every living being, is concerned about many things, above all about those which condition his very existence, such as food and shelter. But man, in contrast to other living beings, has spiritual concerns— cognitive, aesthetic, social, political. Some of them are urgent, often extremely urgent, and each of them as well as the vital concerns can claim ultimacy for a human life or the life of a social group. If it claims ultimacy it demands the total surrender of him who accepts this claim, and it promises total fulfillment even if all other claims have to be subjected to it or rejected in its name" (pp. 1-2).

My personal reading in Tillich doesn't help me define ultimate concern. He illustrates it in part by pointing to the faith of Israel in Yahweh, with Yahweh being the ultimate concern. Tillich though appears to have room for ultimate concern being whatever is of ultimate concern to the person. He did demonstrate some limits on that. For instance, being ultimately concerned on "success" was not ultimate concern. Thus, his position might be akin to what the Alcohol Anonymous movement calls "higher power." (Tillich, 2011).

CARL ROGERS: *Well, that sort of sets off in me a somewhat deeper question. I realize very well that I and many other therapists are interested in the kind of issues that involve the religious worker and the theologian, and yet, for myself, I prefer to put my thinking on those issues in humanistic terms, or to attack those issues through the channels of scientific investigation.*

I felt defensive here. It has not been my observation that Rogers' disciples have been as friendly towards the issues of religion and theology. I have been chastised for asserting religious beliefs by person-centered colleagues. The consequence was finding myself reluctant to deal with these issues in person-centered groups. I have other person-centered colleagues who have reported similar experiences. Several years ago on a person-centered network, I shared this statement: "Faith is a form of knowledge with every bit as much integrity as scientific knowledge. It is just a different paradigm." One of the responses was that I was being arrogant about faith. What occurred to me was that assuming that scientific knowledge is the only way to know is itself arrogant. I have since expanded my own view of what is scientific, and it is not limited to some quantitative or qualitative model.

However, in Rogers' statement I feel I get a glimpse of a variation of demythologizing faith. In this case, Rogers indicated he preferred to use "humanistic terms." My own stance is that humanism when distanced from atheism or non-belief is very compatible with traditional Christianity (I write that knowing that Christianity has been used as a club all too often and violates humanistic principles too). Yet, the compassion of both arenas is very profound.

"What was from the beginning, what we have heard, what we have seen with our eyes, what we have looked at and touched with our hands, concerning the Word of Life — and the life was manifested, and we have seen and testify and proclaim to you the eternal life, which was with the Father and was manifested to us" John 1:1-2 (NASB).

Looks like science to me. The subject or object is different than human behavior, or electrons or black holes, but change the words a little and you have a good scientific statement.

In regard to scientific investigation, I am aware that Rogers was well known for his interest in it. His model was not locked into the frequently used quantitative investigations, but also embraced qualitative style methodologies as well. Research was not just conducted using formal instruments, but also ethnography type protocols as well.

Yet, I perceive limits to what Rogers held regarding scientific investigation. In an example that captures both dismissiveness of asserting faith, and a glimpse of a broader meaning of science the following applies as far as I am concerned.

CARL ROGERS: I guess I have some real sympathy for the modern view that is sort of symbolized in the phrase that "God is dead"; that is, that religion no longer does speak to people in the modern world, and I would be interested in knowing why you tend to put your thinking — which certainly is very congenial to that of a number of psychologists these days — why you tend to put your thinking in religious terminology and theological language.

I have been looking for this as I forgot where I saw it. In fact, the "God is Dead" theology never made a general impact. There is some truth that in the sophisticated industrial country mainline denominations have declined. However, there is no indication "that religion no longer" speaks to "the modern world." Rogers was generalizing. It does though reinforce his own effort to use a different language to address human problems than what was and what still is used to address human problems. It is not and cannot be the new language because others have to adopt it. There are in fact a great many people who have not adopted the new language and they shouldn't have to.

PAUL TILLICH: Now, I think that is a very large question . . .

CARL ROGERS: Yes, it is ...

PAUL TILLICH: . . . and it could take all our time, so I want to confine myself to a few points. First: now the fundamental point is that I believe, metaphorically speaking, man lives not only in the horizontal dimension, namely the relationship of himself as a finite being to other finite beings, observing them and managing them, but he also has in himself something which I call, metaphorically, the vertical line; the line not to a heaven with God and other beings in it, but what I mean with the vertical line is towards something which is not transitory and finite; something which is infinite, unconditional, ultimate — I usually say that.

I want to think that Tillich is speaking in a similar manner here to Rogers regarding the unconditional. Rogers though is about the here and now of relationships where positive regard is a characteristic of relationship. Tillich is in the theological arena speaking of the unconditional as infinite, ultimate, the ultimate concern. The infinite is far reaching and is not limited to human relationships. Still Tillich's words are abstract and while there are those who believe they have a hold on what they mean, I find his position only muddies the water theologically. I haven't a clue what he is talking about as I very seldom use Tillich' jargon.

PAUL TILLICH: Man has an experience in himself that he is more than a piece of finite objects which come and go. He experiences something beyond time and space. I don't speak here – I must emphasize this in speeches again and again – in terms of life after death, or in other symbols which cannot be used in this way anymore, but I speak of the immediate experience of the temporal, of the eternal in the temporal, or of the temporal invaded by the eternal in some moments of our life and of the life together with other people and of the group life.

Surely, the contemporary scientific thinker, and also any disciple influenced by science, would be hard pressed to speak of "life after death." However, for Tillich to assume that there are symbols that cannot be used any more to represent "something beyond time and space" was/is a subjective stance. There are a host of new translations of New Testament materials that still use traditional symbols which have not been abandoned and to which people are relating and accepting.

Tillich did though seem to have a flavor of the whole is greater than the sum of its parts when he said, "Man has an experience in himself that is more than a piece of finite objects which come and go." He is doing this a theologian rather than a psychotherapist. It also seems to me that his position on the experience of the temporal is what can be described as the here and now. This also is often bigger than the person's experience. There are probably infinite events that cannot be consciously grasped by any person in the temporal moment. The human being has some sense of that, while the gorilla or fish does not. In saying that, I can be sure Tillich would make that association and agree with my point as an illustration of his statement.

PAUL TILLICH: Now, that is for me the reason why I try to continue to interpret the great traditional religious symbols as relevant for us: because I know, and that was the other point you made, that they have become largely irrelevant, and that we cannot use them in the way in which they are used still very much in preaching, religious teaching, and liturgies, for people who can live in them, who are not by critical analysis estranged from them, but for those large amounts of people whom you call humanists, we need a translation and interpretation of this symbol, but not, as you seem to indicate, a replacement.

Tillich's position, as stated in the annotation above, reflects his subjective stance. There are uncounted persons who have not found old symbols irrelevant even if there are also uncounted persons who have found those symbols irrelevant. Therefore, some relevancy remains. Tillich though wants to offer alternative expressions, terms, jargon, or symbols that contemporary man may find relevant. Yet, did he? While Tillich remains an intellectual force to deal with, there is no evidence that his ideas, thoughts, interpretations, and/or theology have become mainstream, or that they will. Tillich himself then probably has become more irrelevant despite his attempt to reinterpret symbols of faith and be relevant.

Frankly, when I read Tillich, I tend to see Luther, who has had a far broader impact than Tillich.

I also tend to see in Rogers what I consider Reformed theology even if Rogers' is bouncing off or away from that domain of the Christian faith. For instance, as stated earlier, Rogers sees his approach as one viewing persons in a more positive way than traditional Christianity. I ask, why did he need to make that contrast if he had not been impacted by that traditional Christianity?

PAUL TILLICH: I don't believe that scientific language is able to express the vertical dimension adequately, because it is bound to the relationship of finite things to each other, even in psychology and certainly in all physical sciences. This is the reason why I think we need another language, and this language is the language of symbols and myths; it is a religious language.

I am on the same page with Tillich here. Contemporary scientific jargon even after about 50 years since Tillich made this statement has not offered a language or a paradigm to get at "the vertical dimension adequately." In traditional Christian language, can sinners do that apart from revelation? That paradigm requires another jargon and that is found in the language of faith. Tillich attempted to offer different symbols for faith. Traditional symbols though have remained even as Tillich himself asserted they were/ are irrelevant. Still, surely some have found Tillich's jargon helpful as he still is studied long after his death.

PAUL TILLICH: But we poor theologians, in contrast to you happy psychologists, are in the bad situation that we know the symbols with which we deal have to be reinterpreted and even radically reinterpreted. But I have taken this heavy yoke upon myself and I have decided long ago I will continue to the end with it.

I trust that Tillich was having some fun here. In fact, Rogers himself represents a radical reinterpretation of psychotherapy (Bozarth, 1998).

Both Tillich and Rogers had the honor to continue "to the end with it." They both continue to touch people's lives.

CARL ROGERS: Well, I realized as you were talking, I have a sort of a fantasy of this vertical dimension for me, not going up, but going down.

Rogers does not appear to be willing to let Tillich have this vertical dimension to himself or keep it in the domain of theology. His own demythologizing shows up. I keep in mind Rogers was raised in one of the traditional Christian frameworks (Reformed).

CARL ROGERS: What I mean is this: I feel at times when I'm really being helpful to a client of mine, in those sort of rare moments when there is something approximating an I-Thou relationship between us, and when I feel that something significant is happening, then I feel as though I am somehow in tune with the forces in the universe or that forces are operating through me in regard to this helping relationship that - well, I guess I feel somewhat the way the scientist does when he is able to bring about the splitting of the atom.

Dare I delve into the very language that Tillich asserted was irrelevant. Rogers brings the vertical down into the relationship. In that traditional language from which both diverged, "love your neighbor as yourself" seems relevant to Rogers' position. Also, "Bear one another's burdens, and thereby fulfill the law of Christ" Galatians 6:2 (NASB). These quotes do not overtly reflect Rogers. Yet, I regard them as congruent with what Rogers asserted. Tillich though might have referred to them in his theology or sermons if not in his own work.

CARL *ROGERS: He didn't create it with his own little hands, but he nevertheless put himself in line with the significant forces of the universe and thereby was able to trigger off a significant event, and I feel much the same way, I think, oftentimes, in dealing with a client when I really am being helpful.*

I am aware I have digressed away from Tillich and Rogers efforts into a more traditional or orthodox jargon. The contrast with the old seems important to bring out. Another Biblical theme of awe came to mind as I read what I perceive from Rogers as a theme of awe. "Know that the LORD Himself is God; It is He who has made us, and not we ourselves . . . Psalm 100:3 (NASB). The language of the Psalmist throws the theme into the realms faith and does not reflect secular existentialism or person-centered humanism. It does though indicate the creative aspects of the universe are essentially from another realm, the realm of the creator/God.

PAUL *TILLICH: I am very grateful about what you say. Now, the first words were especially interesting to me, when you said a vertical line has always an up and a down. And you will be interested to hear from me that I am accused very often by my theological colleagues that I speak much too much of down, instead of up, and that is true; when I want to give a name to that with which I am ultimately concerned, then I call it the "ground of being" and ground is, of course, down and not up - so I go with you down. Now the question is, where do we go?*

Here again I had the feeling I could go far away with you when you use the term "universe," forces of the universe, but when I speak of "ground of being," I don't understand this depth of the universe in terms of an addition of all elements in the universe, of all single things, but, as many philosophers and theologians did, the creative ground of the universe, that out of which all these forms and elements come: and I call it the creative ground.

I am very sure that any comment I make here will be puny. I don't have a clue about this up and down image.

Tillich (1957) speaks of the ultimate concern as essentially what traditionally has been called faith. In essence, the "ground of being" is what has traditionally been called God. The ultimate concern then is a focus on the ground of being. It would be more than the being, but is the counter to non-being, that which might traditionally has been seen as Creator (Tillich 1957a). The term carries with it the sense of "divine self-manifestation" (Tillich, 1951).

PAUL TILLICH: *And this was the second point in which I was glad. This creative ground can be experienced in everything which is rooted in the creative ground. For instance, in a person-to-person encounter – and I had without being an analyst, but in many forms of encounters with human beings, very similar experiences to those you had – there is something present which transcends the limited reality of the Thou and the Ego of the other one and of myself, and I sometimes called it at special moments the presence of the holy, in a nonreligious conversation. That I can experience and have experienced, and I agree with you.*

I found myself wondering here if Tillich moved more towards what Rogers was addressing, the person to person interaction, or as Rogers said, the relationship. Tillich seems to address it as something sacred, "holy." He spoke of the "nonreligious conversation" but puts a theological twist to this "conversation.

He does not appear to insist that the nonreligious be grasped as holy by the nonreligious. It is rather Tillich's take as a theologian.

PAUL TILLICH: *Then finally, there was your third point about the scientists, and I often told my scientist friends that they follow strictly the principle formulated classically by Thomas Aquinas, the great medieval theologian: If you know something, then you know something about God. And I would agree with this statement – and therefore these men also have an experience of what I like to call the vertical line, down and perhaps also up, although what they do in splitting atoms is discovering and managing finite relations to each other.*

This feels like a broad statement on knowing, that knowing says something about revelation of God. It is something of a grasping of God.

Surely, this is not at all related to anything like Rogers. Rogers does not theologize the personal relationship, nor does he theologize science and knowing. Thus, Tillich ventures into a paradigm that Rogers does not go.

CARL *ROGERS: I'd like to shift to another topic that has been of interest to me and I suspect may be of interest to you. This is the question of what constitutes the optimal person. In other words, what is it that we're working toward, whether in therapy or in the area of religion? For myself, I have a rather simple definition, yet one which I think has a good many implications. I feel that I'm quite pleased in my work as a therapist if I find that my client and I, too, are – if we are both moving toward what I think of as greater openness to experience. If the individual is becoming more able to listen to what's going on within himself, more sensitive to the reactions he's having to a given situation, if he's more accurately perceptive of the world around him - both the world of reality and the world of relationships – then I think my feeling is I will be pleased. That's the direction I would hope we would move, because then he will be in the process - first of all, he will be in the process all the time. This isn't a static kind of a goal for an individual, and he will be in the process of becoming more fully himself. He'll also be realistic, in the best sense, in that he's realistic about what is going on within himself, as well as realistic about the world, and I think he will also be in the process of becoming more social simply because one of the elements which he can't help but actualize in himself is the need and desire for closer human relationships; so for me, this concept of openness to experience describes a good deal of what I would hope to see in the more optimal person, whether we're talking about the person who emerges from therapy, or the development of a good citizen, or whatever. I wonder if you would have any comments on that or on your own point of view in that area.*

I cannot point to Rogers' critics on this. When Rogers addressed the Fully Functioning Person (1961), he was not limiting his description to some ideal person that can only be reached by a handful of super-humans. Something of these characteristics above are obtainable by every human being in relationship to their person experiences. Every person can function at his/her fullest, though this differs from person to person.

My favorite illustration from Rogers is the potatoes in the potato cellar which under adverse conditions still manage to throw out appendages consistent with the genetic codes that enable potatoes to be potatoes and to strive to create new potatoes. I have been amazed many times by human beings who even in comas still manage to function within the limits of the problem that triggered that coma. I have even seen people on their death bed, snap out of a coma, tend to some details in the life, then slip back into the coma and die. Rogers never espoused that his observation on human potential were without limits and that all people have, inherently some ability to function at the level of genius or have extremely high levels of self-awareness, etc. He just found that in counseling and psychotherapy that clients tended to move in directions, in part described above. His other works including (1951, 1961, 1980), describe this further.

PAUL TILLICH: Yes, there are two questions in this. The one is the way – namely the openness – and the other is the aim. It is, of course, not a static aim, not a dynamic aim, but it's an aim. Let me speak to both points: the openness is a word which is very familiar to myself because there are many questions a theologian is asked, and which can be answered only by the concept of openness or opening up. I will give you two examples. The one example is the function of classical symbols and symbols generally. I always used to answer: "Symbols open up, they open up reality and they open up something in us." If this word were not forbidden in the university today, I would call it something in our soul, but you know as a psychologist, as somebody who deals with the soul, that the word "soul" is forbidden in academic contexts.

Goodness, this was Paul Tillich speaking about a taboo. Freedom of speech didn't apply!

PAUL TILLICH: *But that's what symbols do, and they do it not only to individuals, but they do it also to groups and usually only through groups to individuals — so that's the one thing where I use the word "open." This seems to me one of the main functions, perhaps the main function of symbols — namely to open up. Then another use of the word "open" is that I am asked, "Now what can I do to experience God or to get the Divine Spirit?" or things like that. My answer is, "The only thing you can do is keep yourselves open. You cannot force God down, you cannot produce the Divine Spirit in yourselves, but what you can do is open yourselves, to keep yourselves open for It."*

A little Pauline and Lutheran theology sneaking out. "But the righteousness based on faith says, "Do not say in your heart, 'Who will ascend into heaven?'" (that is, to bring Christ down) "or 'Who will descend into the abyss?'" (that is, to bring Christ up from the dead). But what does it say? "The word is near you, in your mouth and in your heart" (that is, the word of faith that we proclaim); Romans 10:6-8 (ESV). Luther (1959) "none of us has life himself, or anything else that has been of himself, or anything else that has been mentioned here or can be mentioned, nor can he by himself preserve any of them, however small and unimportant. All this is comprehended in the word 'Creator'" (p. 56).

PAUL TILLICH: *This is, of course, in your terminology, a particular experience, but we must keep open for all experiences. So I would agree very much with the way which you have described. I would even believe that in all experiences, there is a possibility of having an ultimate experience.*

It appears to me that Tillich makes a step towards Rogers' position here on openness towards experiences of persons.

PAUL TILLICH: *Then, the aim: now, the aim is the many folds we discussed. Perhaps we could agree about realization of our true self, bringing into actuality what is essentially given to us; or, when I speak in religious symbolism, I could say: "To become the way in which God sees us, in all our potentialities."*

Rogers (1961) wrote of the self that one truly is. This self is accepting of experiences, ideas, thoughts, etc. Some of Rogers characteristics of this include: movement 1) "away from facades," 2) "away from 'oughts'", 3) "away from meeting expectations", 4) away from pleasing others (pp. 167-170). In my own personal experience, I have lost count of the number of times I have gotten in trouble for having this attitude including even being told I am a legend in my own mind. Society does not encourage this behavior even as a popular song contained the words "I did it my way." Rogers supplemented the above position by asserting that as the person moves away, he/she also moves towards a set of behaviors: 1) "Towards self-direction, 2) "toward being process" (Rogers acknowledged describing this is problematic), 3) "toward being complexity", 4) "toward being open to experience", 5) "toward acceptance of others", 6). "toward acceptance of self" (pp. 170-175). I don't see rebellion or laissez faire in this, neither is their room for pulling power plays on or suppression of others.

Tillich's openness is related to the "New Being" (the Christ in traditional Christian language) who enables the person to the creature God (the Ground of Being) brought into existence. This creature however is estranged from the full grasp of this but moves towards completion via ultimate concern (faith).

PAUL TILLICH: *And what that now practically is, is the next and very important question. You also indicated something of this: namely, to become social. I think this is a part of a larger concept. I would call it love, in the sense of the Greek word agape, which is a particular word in the New Testament, and which means that love which is described by Paul in I Corinthians 13, and which accepts the other as a person and then tries to reunite with him and to overcome the separation, the existential separation, which exists between men and men. Now, with this aim, I would agree; but I would add, of course, since I speak also in terms of the vertical dimension, that it is the keeping to that dimension to maintain in the faith into an ultimate meaning of life, and the absolute and unconditional seriousness of this direction of this ultimate aim of life. So when I shall speak now in popular terms, which is very dangerous always, I would say: faith and love are the two concepts which are necessary, but faith not in the sense of beliefs but in the sense of being related to the ultimate, and love not in the sense of any sentimentality, but in a sense of affirming the other person and even one's own person, because I believe with Augustine, Erich Fromm, and others, that there is a justified self-affirmation and self-acceptance. I wouldn't use the term "self-love" – that's too difficult – but self-affirmation and self-acceptance, one of the most difficult things to reach.*

"If there is an arena where Rogers, Tillich, and traditional Christianity and other faiths can come together it is here." While Rogers used the term "unconditional positive regard" from 1957 until his death, Tillich uses the word "love." The premier koine Greek word from the New Testament is "agape." Granted there is abstraction, lack of clarity, and ambiguity in all these words or phrases. It probably amounts to splitting hair to get at the differences.

It would be hard to assert that either Tillich or Rogers did not believe that considering this positive experience, theologically or humanistically, people tend to grow, change, and have better lives. It is in this area that Rogers' concept of incongruence, and Tillich's concept of estrangement are engaged. If incongruence and estrangement aren't over come in the here and now in the presence of love or unconditional positive regard, certainly its influence offers opportunity for something new and different to happen. Surely, love or positive regard is a step up from those incongruent or estranged experiences where love or positive regard is at low levels.

CARL ROGERS: Well, I find that I like it best when you become concrete; that is, when you put it in terms of faith and love. Those can be very abstract concepts which can have all kinds of different meanings, but putting it in the concrete – yes, I do feel that the person does have to gain a real appreciation of or liking of himself, if he is going to affirm himself in a healthy and useful fashion.

I cannot recall seeing Rogers say "I do feel that the person does have to gain a real appreciation of or liking of himself, if he is going to affirm himself . . . ." I have heard uncounted person-centered therapist assert that the positive regard of the therapist may indeed be realized by clients. Rogers statement is rather logical. Healthy people probably do have real appreciation for themselves,

CARL ROGERS: There's one other corollary to this notion of being open to experience that we might explore a bit, too. To me, the individual who is reasonably open to his experience is involved in a continuous valuing process; that is, I think that – I realize that I've sort of dropped the notion of values in the conventional sense of there being certain values which you could list, and that kind of thing – but it does seem to me that the individual who is open to his experience is continually valuing each moment and valuing his behavior in each moment, as to whether it is related to his own self-fulfillment, his own actualization, and that it's that kind of valuing process that to me makes sense in the mature person.

This is consistent with points presented above from Rogers (1961). I would only add that openness to experience and having real appreciation for one's self, does not mean that these are pain free. I may be very open to grasping that I feel anxious from time to time and appreciating or at least claiming that my anxiety is mine. This doesn't make the anxiety less intense. It might be more intense, though I am convinced people who are open to their feelings and experiences and appreciate them for what they are, get through them faster.

CARL ROGERS: It also makes sense in a world where the whole situation is changing so rapidly that I feel that ordinary lists of values are probably not as appropriate or meaningful as they were in periods gone by.

If they were changing fast in 1965, we know we cannot even keep up with the new technology, advances, and gathering of data before the newest device comes out. As I write this, there are overt conflicts in Syria, Libya, Israel, Palestine, Iran, Iraq, and Afghanistan. These are just in the Mid-East. Views and perspectives are clashing during change and it ain't pretty in all circumstances and hard to value under the realities that people are killed in the conflicts of changing ideals.

PAUL *TILLICH: Yes. Now I am an outspoken critic of the philosophy of values, so I certainly agree with you. I replace this thing by my concept of agape, or love - namely, love which is listening.*

In 1965, Jackie DeShannon sang the words of Hal David and Burt Bacharach's "What the World Needs Now is Love." That has not changed. A person-centered colleague during an interview not long before her death a few years ago said, "The world is going to hell." This statement came from a person adhering the person-centered premise that people can be trusted and are basically good.

Both Tillich (love - agape), and Rogers (unconditional positive regard) espoused "attitudes" (for lack of a better word) that if universally adhered to would make the world a better place. Unfortunately, all it takes is one act of hostility to spoil powerful love and caring. It does not seem to work the other way. Tillich though takes his concept from the theological domain of faith and includes in that the psychological. I cannot say that Rogers affirms that his concept of unconditional positive regard is anything but psycho-social, though he would have and probably did affirm there are many people of faith who have taken unconditional positive regard into their disciplines.

PAUL *TILLICH: I call it listening love, which doesn't follow abstract valuations, but which is related to the concrete situation, and out of its listening to this very moment gains its decision for action and its inner feeling of satisfaction and even joy or dissatisfaction and bad conscience.*

Surely Rogers concept of empathy coupled with unconditional positive regard is compatible with Tillich's "listening love." And I cannot help but believe that Tillich's "inner feeling of satisfaction and joy" represents something of the experience of Rogers' "self that one truly is" as does openness to what Tillich called "dissatisfaction and bad conscience."

CARL *ROGERS: I like that phrase because I think it could be a listening within, a listening to oneself, as well as a listening love for the other individual. . .*

On a tour of the weight room of the Mississippi State baseball team a few years ago, I saw a sign at the exit: "Attitude is Everything." Rogers person-centered approach is the attitude. It indeed is about listening within, to oneself, and to the other person.

PAUL *TILLICH: Yes, when I say listening to the situation, I mean the situation is constituted out of everything around me and myself; so, listening love is always listening to both sides.*

Tillich is not limited to the person-centered jargon. I wonder if that itself makes him more person-centered than Rogers and adherents to the "Rogerian" approach can allow themselves to be. The person-centered approach surely is bigger and broader than espoused by Rogers (Cain, 2010). As a person separate from Rogers' pilgrimage, Tillich is presenting a stance that "listening love" is important.

CARL *ROGERS: I feel we're not very far apart in our thinking about this value approach;*

To my knowledge these two never interacted with each other previously. I saw no indication that Tillich saw Rogers' work or vice versa.

CARL *ROGERS: I thought we might be further apart than we seem to be. But, one other instance: I feel that the small infant is a good example of the valuing process that is going on continuously. He isn't troubled by the concepts and standards that have been built up for adults, and he's continually valuing his experience as either making for his enhancement or being opposed to that actualization.*

I have no reason to believe Rogers was correct in this assessment. I think the infant experiences what he/she experiences and may experience it as bad and thus scream, or as good and thus coo. There just aren't words connected to the experience.

PAUL TILLICH: Now, this valuation, of course, would be not an intellectual valuation, but an evaluation with his whole being . . .

A brief glimpse of separation between these two?

CARL ROGERS: I think of it as an organismic valuing process.

Maybe not such separation.

PAUL TILLICH: That means a reaction of his whole being, and I certainly believe that it is an adequate description.

I don't.

With Tillich's remarks the dialogue comes to an end. They would never see each other again. Paul Tillich died not long after this interaction. October 22, 1965. Carl Rogers died February 4, 1987. I have one letter from Rogers which I received just weeks before he died.

References

Bozarth, J. (1998). *Person-centered therapy: A revolutionary paradigm.* Ross-on-Wye: PCCS Books.

Cain, D. (2010). *Person-centered psychotherapies.* Washington, D.C.: American Psychological Association.

Luther, M. (1959). The Large Catechism of Martin Luther. Fortress Press.

Rogers (1951). *Client centered therapy.* Boston: Houghton Mifflin.

Rogers, C. R. (1961). *On becoming a person.* Boston: Houghton Mifflin.

Rogers, C. R. (1980). *A way of being.* Boston: Houghton Mifflin.

Tillich, P. (1951). Systematic Theology, Vol. 1. Three volumes in one. Chicago: University of Chicago Press.

Tillich, P. (1957). *Dynamics of faith*. New York. HarperCollins.

Tillich, P. (1957a). Systematic Theology, Vol. 2. Three volumes in one. Chicago: University of Chicago Press.

Tillich, Paul (2011). *Dynamics of faith* (Perennial Classics) (p. 120). HarperCollins. Kindle Edition.

The Unknown Rogers:

Glances from Afar

I am not presenting unknown material about Rogers, some information dug up in an obscure location. Rather, the unknown Rogers is the person I never met personally in face to face interactions. There is an uncounted number of us in that category.

I believe I just missed meeting Carl Rogers. In 1987, the Warm Springs Person-Centered Workshop began. Several students in the Counseling and Counseling Psychology program at the University of Georgia participated in that workshop. A handful helped organize it. I was not an organizer, but I felt I was more of a cheer-leader.

It was anticipated that contributors to the approach including Nat Raskin and Barbara Brodley among others would participate. We did not anticipate Carl Rogers being able to attend as it was rumored he was ill. As it turned out he died just a few weeks before the 1st Annual Warm Springs event.

There was some grieving from those that knew him and worked him through the years. I even had a fantasy about offering a memorial event. However, I didn't work up the courage to offer it.

I felt I was a new kid on the block, and it seemed presumptuous to make such an offer.

The previous summer I attended a meeting of the ADPCA (the Association for the Development of the Person-Centered Approach). Rogers was unable to attend that either.

I did manage to write him a letter just a few months before he died, regarding an article in the Person-Centered Review. Comparing his view to that of Kohut, he summarized his own stance. ". . . Seeing as essentially positive in nature – is profoundly radical. It flies in the face of traditional psychoanalysis, runs counter to the Christian tradition, and is opposed to the philosophy of most institutions, including our educational institutions. In psychoanalytic theory our core is seen as untamed, wild, destructive. In Christian theology we are 'conceived in sin,' and evil by nature. In our institutions the individual is seen as untrustworthy. Persons must be guided, corrected, disciplined, punished, so that they will not follow the pathway set by their nature" (Roger, 1986).

My Letter

July 17, 1986

Dear Dr. Rogers:

I was interested in your comment in the May 1986 Person—Centered Review, "seeing the human organism as essentially positive in nature — is profoundly radical. It flies in the face of traditional psychoanalysis, runs counter to the Christian tradition, . . . In Christian theology we are 'conceived in sin,' and evil by nature." This statement is as gross a misunderstanding of the heart of Christianity as any misunderstanding Christianity has had of your theory. While it is true that a theology of sin is a significant part of Christianity, the basic assumption is not that humankind is conceived in sin. The basic assumption is that the human being was and is created in the image of God. Even when John Calvin focused on the "detestable" nature of sin, he found it to be detestable because he believed sin had brought about a distortion of the true self that God had intended each person to be. Calvin even acknowledges that in spite of the profound corruption of sin the image of God shines through. Thus, for Calvin to know one's self is to know God and of course vice versa.

There is no doubt in my mind that Calvin, Wesley and many other theologians would agree that being created in the image of God is to be forward moving, self—directive, constructive, realistic, and trustworthy. Calvin and Wesley of course used terms such as holy and pure to reflect the notion of being made in the image of God. The anathema concerning sin is the distortion of these qualities, qualities which remain in spite of any distortions caused by sin.

Quite frankly I see your theory only incompatible with those who have become alarmed by sin and have let their concepts of sin blind them to tremendous potentials of the true self. Still your own theory acknowledges a distortion of the self. Christianity just pushes toward a focus beyond nature as we know it. Instead of incongruence with one's self on a psychological realm, Christianity talks about an incongruence with one's self on a theological realm. Instead of having one's self and self—concept in harmony, Christianity talks about having one's self in harmony with the ultimate self (God). Christianity also claims that the ultimate self entered our world in Jesus Christ and that this Christ once again reminds us of our basic nature, being created in the image of God.

The focus in Christianity has been on evil, sinful humankind, but this probably does more to illustrate the problem of sin than it does to bring the heathen pagans to their knees. The true focus of Christianity is the creation and the tremendous mechanisms which reflect the creative processes inherent within the universe. Christianity is ultimately an optimistic religion, even though it has believers who reflect a pessimistic, self-righteous, hostile attitude.

Therefore, I am arguing that your theory does not fly in the face of Christianity. However, it does fly in the face of our misconceptions and distortions of Christianity. It is a shame, however, that the secular world should have to remind the faithful of the Imago Dei even when that is not the intent or purpose of the secular world.

I hope these thoughts remind you that there are many within the Christian faith who do not hold that humankind is evil and wicked in nature, but that God created human beings in the Imago Dei, and it was and is good.

Very truly yours,
Douglas W. Bower

I thought so highly of myself for writing that letter. As I look at it now, it has an element of hubris. Carl Rogers, raised in the Reformed Tradition, knew these things.

I was excited to get a response. I misread the response. My recollection was that Rogers indicated he had not thought about these things the way I did. So, I patted myself on the back.

I misplaced the material. In fact, I thought I had carelessly disposed of the computer file which contained it. I used a Tandy desktop computer with a floppy disk to write the material. I gave it away to an elementary school nearby as I upgraded technology. The staff was trying to catch up and gladly took that computer. I disposed of all my floppy disks, including the disk with the letter to Rogers.

Then several years later, as I was going through my files, I found I had made a hard copy of my letter. I also found Rogers' response. On re-reading it, it didn't strike me in the same positive manner that I remembered.

Carl Rogers' Brief Eesponse:

Center for Studies of the Person
July 22, 1986

Dear Douglas Bower,

Thank you for your informative letter. I am well aware that many Christians do have a positive view of human nature and I was particularly interested in your comments on Calvin.

I wonder if you wouldn't agree that the Fundamentalists wing of Christianity goes further than your letter and does feel that man is conceived in sin.

One sentence in your letter seems contradictory to your main point - - "The focus in Christianity has been on evil, sinful humankind" - - It seems to me that was what I was talking about.

Thank you for your letter and I wish you well in your work.

Sincerely,
Carl R. Rogers, Ph.D.
Resident Fellow

On re-reading his response, the following word popped into my mind: Gotcha! "The focus in Christianity has been on evil, sinful humankind." In short, I failed to get at my point and cluttered it. My point was not clear. Even Christianity got too wrapped up in seeing the human being as totally depraved. It still fails to highlight that human beings were/are created in the Imago Dei. My point was that man was created in the image of God and declared good. Our basic human nature is good, not evil. That "good" nature remains, distorted, but still remains. Human beings are in a state of incongruence or estranged from the very nature that still exists. The Imago Dei has not disappeared. It has not been replaced. The alienation and the nature exist together. I failed to communicate adequately that point when I wrote the letter.

Over the years, theologically, I felt that incongruence was part of the essence of sin. The person gets out of sync with the self. The self has not disappeared. Thus, the anathema of sin was that the sinner is out of touch with being a creature of God. The consequences are devastating. In essence, human beings are created both in the Imago Dei and the state of sin, a broken, estranged condition, not just a wickedness of rebellion and defiance. In fact, Rogers was right, I illustrated his point further even as I tried to highlight human beings being created good and holding the Imago Dei. Still, being created in the Imago Dei came first in the Creation story. So, I still assert the basic element is that human beings were created good and that still remains. It has just that it has been distorted. Thus, we come into that as well. Rogers though didn't or wouldn't go there. I did and do.

With more dialogue with Rogers perhaps we could have gotten to that. My brief inadequate letter to him was presumptuous and awkwardly stated.

However, Rogers was far too optimistic for me regarding the human condition. There, in fact, is not a lot of evidence that human behavior has improved since Rogers presented his nondirective ideals.

He did though influence me putting more hope in the personal resources people have which they can use to creatively change their lives. I have not though abandoned a concept of sin which, in my mind, all too often thwarts that creativity. The problems of "bad behavior" are not just from the negative forces of society but come from within. Rogers didn't seem to get at the later. If people have personal resources that they can use for good, how is it that they don't cut through the negative forces that suppress and oppress people? How is it they do not help themselves and all too often act in self-destructive ways? How is it they often hurt others?

I hardly ever hear Person-Centered colleagues argue for the goodness of human beings any more. It does though seem to me that those espousing the theory and practice assert that the basic conditions of the approach do make it easier for people to move in constructive ways. In essence, a principle of clients always doing their best still remains. I have flabbergasted colleagues by pointing out that suggests that people don't choose not to do their best.

Basic Stance: Self Actualization and the Necessary and Sufficient Conditions

I define self-actualization as a multi-factorial ontological process whereby the person, all that he/she is or can be, becomes real or actual. It is made up of the composite creative factors that come into play that make it possible for the person to live and exist.

Some of those creative factors involved the physiological aspects of what makes us human beings. These include DNA, molecules, cells, and organs. Important to this is brain, a complex bio-physiological entity that monitors a great deal of the organism, its experiences, and feelings. Of the function of the brain is the ability to think and communicate via non-verbal and verbal language.

In a section below, I will address the concept of the Fully Functioning Person which I believe shows the ideal of the self-actualizing person.

Somehow, someway, the ideal mental part of the organism can go awry. When it does, the person may feel mental anguish. It is here that various theories and practices of differing psychotherapies were triggered in efforts to help. The Person-Centered approach is one of those.

Amid the realities of the state of human beings who are troubled, Rogers presented the "facilitative psychological attitudes." He did so in various ways. His (1989/1957) work is basic. "For constructive personality change to occur, it is necessary that these conditions exist and continue for an extended period.

1). Two persons are in psychological contact.
2). The first, whom we shall term the client, is in a state of incongruence, being vulnerable or anxious.
3). The second person, whom we shall term the therapist, is congruent or integrated in the relationship.
4). The therapist experiences unconditional positive regard for the client.
5). The therapist experiences an empathic understanding of the client's internal frame of reference and endeavors to communicate this experience to the client.
6). The communication to the client of the therapist's empathic understanding and unconditional positive regard is to a minimal degree achieved." (Rogers, 1989/1957, p. 221).

Exegesis and Annotation

There are limits in words. The symbols of word don't capture wholeness of ideas. Thus, this aspect of the project might generate questions of meaning, or clarification. One takes risks in presenting notions. I am doing so now.

I also take a position that exegesis is engaging what is presented. Thus, I will use quotes with my comments. Rogers is better at speaking for himself than someone else. This prevents liberties in regard to annotations, and thus limits eisegesis.

I'll start with "constructive personality change."

Is it about an introvert becoming an extrovert? Is it about a person who experiences chronic depression or anxiety, finding ways to experience joy and security? The answer to both questions and others like it, might be, yes. It might also be, no. What if I learn to respect being an introvert? What if I understand that every person gets depressed, and thus in learning to accept my depression, I also raise my opinion of it, and thus diminish its trap. I don't stop ever not getting depressed, but I include joy in the next moment. Or better yet, I discover I have significant control in my experiences. I find my personal resources, which are both external and internal, important in managing my experiences.

Rogers' (1951) "characteristic change" in therapy is useful to speak for describing "constructive personality change." This might involve change:

1). "In Type of Material Presented"
   a). "The individual first tended to talk about his problems and his symptoms for a majority of the time, this type of talk tended to be replaced, as therapy progressed, by insightful statements showing some understanding of relationships between his past and present behavior and between current behaviors" (pp. 132-133).

b). "It was observed that while the client, at the outset of therapy, seemed to voice mostly negative feelings, there appeared to be a change in a positive direction (pp. 133-134).

c). "The client's exploration revolves first around the various aspects of the problem, but gradually the concern is more and more with self. What kind of person am I? What are my real feelings? What is my real self?" (p. 135).

d). "Not only is there movement from symptoms to self, but from environment to self and from others to self" (p. 135).

e). "The content of the conversation is from material which has always been available in awareness, to material which until therapy has not been available to conscious consideration" (p. 135).

f). "Another change in material is from past to present" (p. 135).

2). "In Perception of and Attitude Toward Self" (p. 136).

a). This perception tended to move from negative to positive. "At the conclusion of therapy there are more positively toned self-references than negative" (p. 137).

3). In "movement toward Awareness of Denied Experience" (p. 147).

a). "Bringing into awareness of experiences of which heretofore the client has not been conscious" (p. 147). My take on this is "How are you feeling?" which may be answered, "I don't know," becomes "I am feeling . . . ." The "I don't know" statement is either defensiveness or incongruence, that is the client really doesn't know at the conscious level. An indication of "change" occurs when the client can get at the "I don't know" aspects of his/her experience.

4). In "characteristic Movement in the Valuing Process" (p. 149).

    a). "The client comes to realize that he is trying to live by what others think, that he not being his real self, and he is less and less satisfied with this situation" (p. 149). A 2017 Meme that circulated on Facebook captured something of the initial problem. "The person who tries to keep everyone happy and always cares for everyone is always the most lonely person. Strange but true." The client moves towards assertiveness and may embrace the views of others in a different manner. In short, the client looks out after his/her own interest, which might mean doing something he or she does not want to, because the price of not doing so appears too high.

5). "In Personality Structure and Organization" (p. 172).

    a). I am not an advocate regarding personality change. So, I can't make a case for this point. Rogers though asserted the following: "This change appears to be in the direction of: an increased unification and integration of personality; a lessened degree of neurotic tendency; a decreased amount of anxiety; a greater degree of acceptance of self and of emotionality as a part of self; increased objectivity in dealing with reality; more effective mechanisms for dealing with stress-creating situations; more constructive feelings and attitudes; and a more effective intellectual functioning. On the basis of limited evidence, it would appear that these personality changes are relatively permanent, often continuing in the directions already described" (p. 178).

    Is this personality change or behavioral change? I lean towards calling this description, behavioral change. To me an illustration of personality change is an introvert becoming an extrovert, or a sociopath becoming more sensitive to the experiences of others.

6). "In Behavior" (p. 179) paraphrased:
   a). Discusses plans (p. 180).
   b). More mature and responsible behavior (p. 180).
   c). Psychological tension decreases (p. 181).
   d). Lowering of defensive behaviors (p. 182).
   e). Able to better tolerate frustration (p. 183).
   f). Practical behaviors like reading and job performance improve (pp. 184-185).

This material is not a research project. I have presented claims. Rogers provided support from the research of his time. Like all research is it subject to reflection including accepting its accuracy.

Now for the necessary and sufficient conditions that allegedly enable "constructive personality change."

Psychological Contact

For a long time, I felt that empathy and psychological contact went hand in hand. That is, if I have empathic experiences with someone else, I am in psychological contact with that person.

However, I no longer view the psychological contact as automatic, even if I can have the experience of empathy. I assert that empathy might inform me that I don't have the psychological contact.

The point Rogers made is that 2 persons are in contact, not just one. The therapist may indeed have empathic experiences in relationship to the client, but that does not mean the client has psychological contact with the therapist/counselor.

I began to rethink this in relationship to connections I have made supporting high school sporting programs which I will address momentarily.

For years as a counselor/therapist there were clients of all sorts that I felt uncomfortable with. I don't remember getting at that in supervision during my training. My interpretation of that experience was I was simply not a good therapist. I did get at it in therapy as a client. It was consistent with my self-view of not being good enough.

I know consider that view incorrect, not just because it was a personality quirk, but because there is an element about therapy I didn't get. That element is relationship, rapport or connection. I thought I got the words from Irwin Yalom's (1995) work on Group Therapy. On re-visiting that work, I don't believe I got there. Yalom's (2001) "The Gift of Therapy" does have a brief chapter called "Engage the Patient." "Nothing takes precedence over the care and maintenance of my relationship to the patient . . ." (p. 11). That doesn't seem to do justice to the "ah-ha" I had. Sidney Jourard (1971) said, "The amount of personal information that one person is willing to disclose to another appears to be an index of the 'closeness' of the relationship . . ." (p. 13).

These though weren't helpful to me. Rogers' concept "psychological contact" wasn't either. What was helpful was this.

I had been involved with a high school baseball program. The coach received a new position at a nearby high school. He invited me to go with him. However, I declined saying I had seen these young men grow up. I wanted to continue to support them. The new head coach had been on staff and asked me to remain.

During "summer ball" his younger players, under an assistant coach, lost badly. The opponent scored over 20 runs in the second game of double header. After the game, the new head coach came out of the stands and began to berate the players. He then made them run and run and run and run. Players were falling on their knees begging for him to stop. He kept running them.

I was watching this and getting madder and madder as I said two things to myself: Surely he will stop soon, and Doug, you need to say something. He didn't stop and I didn't say anything.

In my anger, I took my gear down to my car. I came back up to the field and he was still running them.

After he finished, he scolded them. Then he made them jog to the right field foul pole and back.

When he came up to me, he said, "We are going to make this team into a baseball team."

I said, "Coach, I hope so, but that was absolutely the worst case of coaching I have ever seen. Don't you ever do that again."

I stormed off.

The next day I went to the Athletic Director and complained.

At the end of summer ball, he did it again with an older group. Now they took better care of themselves and one of the players said, "Thank you coach for getting us in shape after the last game." But they managed to jog instead of run until they were sick.

I again went to the Athletic Director who was very defensive this time.

Just before the regular season I was asked not to remain involved with the team. The psychological contact, if had been there was gone. Rapport was shattered.

I called the former coach and asked if his invitation still stood. It did. I joined his new team in time to help him get started.

This led to involvement with a new football team as the chemistry involving the football team at the other school had also deteriorated. I felt disconnected with the old team as well.

My "ah-ha" came with the new football team.

After practice one day, the head coach asked if anyone had something to say. I knew some of the football players because they played baseball. A couple of the coaches also coached baseball. So, I was not a stranger to the program.

I raised my hand. The coach called on one person after and other. He kept passing me by. Finally, still keeping my hand up, he called on me. He seemed reluctant to do so.

I said something. I don't remember what. Essentially, it was about not taking it for granted what others believed in the team and its abilities and to work hard anyway.

Afterwards, the coach called me aside and said, "Doc, I know you have been a part of the athletic program over here. But the next time you have something to say, ask me first." He had just extended an invitation, then acknowledged me allowing me to speak. This though was followed with, you aren't welcome to speak under these conditions. I felt very disconnected. If there had been rapport (psychological contact), it was gone.

"OK," I said. I had a sick empty feeling inside. I was stunned. I had not felt connected with the football program.

So, I left, going to a football team in another county to which the team had invited me. I got many chances to share thoughts and encouragement. The psychological contact remained. I enjoyed associating with a team having a very successful season. The other two teams had losing seasons.

In that, my "ah-ha" was rapport, or chemistry, or relationship, is important. It cannot be assumed. Behavior itself does not guarantee it. Offering care or help, or whatever, doesn't guarantee psychological contact will be present. It is a separate condition or experience.

That is what Rogers was getting at. Psychological contact is that rapport, connection, chemistry, or relationship. Just because I am the professional counselor does not mean it will happen. Just because I have knowledge on how to do counseling, doesn't mean it will happen. It is a spontaneous experience. It is a mutual experience between client and counselor.

I am prepared to say that the establishment of this rapport not only comes easier with some clients than with others, but that some people can do it one on one, or a small group or with the masses more often than others. I don't do it well with individuals. I do it better with small groups of 4 - 12. Others do it better in larger groups. Rogers, I submit, did it with the masses becoming a recognized figure. People who never met him, called him "Carl."

What does it look like? I turn to an one-on-one experience to illustrate it, sitting on the front porch with your best friend.

After 2 years I visited with an old friend I met while I was studying in college. We both attended the same Church. The relationship has lasted 48 years.

We had lunch together at a restaurant in a community located half way between us.

During our lunch we talked about a lot of stuff, family, recollections, stresses, and a great deal about our concerns about education. She is a kindergarten teacher a few years from retirement. I am, at this writing, a member of the Board of Education in my county. We also talked about religion and our stances on the denomination to which we still both belong.

I would speak for a time. Kathy would speak for a time. My words triggered thoughts with her. Her words triggered thoughts with me. We both expressed ourselves. We both heard each other. If we were confused about a point, we asked about it. We also shared our differences on a variety of issues.

Suddenly 2 hours was up. Nothing else was going on in the world. We were focused. We concentrated on each other's presence and words. Time flew by.

I am convinced that is what happens in good therapy. The focus and concentration are such that nothing else is going on in the world. The difference is the therapist doesn't spend as much energy expressing his or her ideas, thoughts, and experiences. Instead, that energy is channeled into hearing, really hearing.

And then suddenly the session is over.

Incongruence of the Client

A brief description of this is found in Rogers' words: the client is "vulnerable and anxious."

Myself, I don't believe that being "vulnerable and anxious" is just a state of incongruence. We are all vulnerable, and daily living is full of potential circumstances that can stir anxiety.

Rogers (1989/1957) presented incongruence saying, "It refers to a discrepancy between the actual experience of the organism and the self picture of the individual insofar as it represents that experience"

(p. 222). Rogers associated vulnerability with having little awareness of his/her incongruence. That triggers for me recollections of the old Freudian notion of repression where those experience show up in dreams and the client doesn't make connections with the dream and his/her experiences. Or perhaps, severe suppression, where the client essentially stuffed experiences for any number of reasons and they are just outside of one's grasp. This though is not particularly consistent with person-centered philosophy which does not use, nor gravitate towards the Freudian or psycho-dynamic model. With the incongruent person, experiences are not incorporated into awareness and are denied (Rogers, 1961).

In the (1961) work Rogers gave a brief illustration of incongruence. "To pick an easily recognizable example take the man who becomes angrily involved in a group discussion. His face flushes, his tone communicates anger, he shakes his finger at his opponent. Yet when a friend says 'well, let's not get angry about this,' he replies, with evident sincerity and surprise, 'I'm not angry! I don't have any *feeling* about this at all! I was just pointing out the logical facts'" (pp. 339-340).

This example is far more down to earth to me then Rogers's definition of incongruence.

A basic understanding of the person-centered approach that I have adopted holds that every person has vast resources that the person can use creatively for growth and change. "Individuals have within themselves vast resources for self-understanding and for altering their self-concepts, basic attitudes, and self-directed behavior" (Rogers, 1980, p. 115). Rogers called that "the central apotheosis of this approach."

Incongruence in my thinking is the state of a person losing touch with, or failing to trust, those resources. The incongruent person does not know how to access or use those resources. Consequently, he/she seeks help, and indeed might feel "vulnerable and anxious" and not know why or what to do about it. I am incongruent, when I am unaware of my personal resources, or lacking trust in those resources. Thus, I may shut down and withdraw when I don't trust my internal or external resources or insist that others "fix" me because I don't trust or am not aware of my own personal resources.

The Congruent Therapist

If "incongruence" is difficult to describe, "congruence" is also. It is probably easy to get at what is wrong with people, and with ourselves. Get involved in social media and it is quickly perceived how much people think others are wrong, maladjusted, mistaken, or troubled.

Suddenly old Transactional Analysis type thoughts came to mind: "I'm OK, you're not OK;" "I'm not OK, you are OK;" "I'm not OK, you're not OK;" and finally the ideal, "I'm OK, You're OK." Is that latter statement a statement about congruence?

I am going briefly address my myth about the congruent person. I shed it years ago, but a description of it remains. The congruent person is stable, organized, confident, well-adjusted, experiences personal peace, joy, and love. The person doesn't experience instability, disorganization, tentativeness, anxiety, fear, or anger.

With that last statement, I have grounds for rejecting my myth about congruence.

I rely on Rogers's (1989/1957) work. In that work he describes congruence this way. "That their condition is that the therapist should be, within the confines of this relationship, a congruent, genuine, integrated person" (pp. 223-224). This spoke to my myth a bit. He continued. "It means that within the relationship he is freely and deeply himself, with his actual experience accurately represented by his awareness of himself. It is the opposite of presenting a façade, either knowingly or unknowingly" (p. 224).

The following helped dispel my myth. "It is not necessary (nor is it possible) that the therapist be a paragon who exhibits this degree of integration, of wholeness, in every aspect of his life . . . Should be clear that this includes being himself even in ways which are not regarded as ideal for psychotherapy" (p. 224).

Rogers (1961) wrote, "I have found that the more that I can be genuine in the relationship, the more helpful it will be. This means that I need to be aware of my own feelings, insofar as possible, rather than presenting an outward façade of one attitude, while actually holding another attitude at a deeper or unconscious level. Being genuine also involves the willingness to be to express, in my words and my behavior, the various feelings and attitudes which exists in me" (p. 33).

Related to that, Rogers (1980) stated, "I find it very satisfying when I can be real, when I can be close to whatever it is that is going on within me . . . In place the term 'realness' I have sometimes use the word 'congruence.' By this I mean that in my experiencing of this moment is present in my awareness and when what is present in my awareness is present in my communication, and each of these three levels matches or is congruent at such moments I am integrated or whole, I am completely in one piece most of the time, of course, I, like everyone else, exhibit some degree of incongruence" (pp. 14-15).

As far as I am concerned that last sentence scrambles the waters on what congruence is.

I seek now to scramble the waters some more. To do so, I will wrestle with those vast resources mentioned above/

With that, I offer this definition of congruence. Congruence is the personal state of being in touch with one's own vast resources. These resources include: feelings, thoughts, and experiences. Certainly, being aware of one's self, including feeling incongruent is part of this stance. In this awareness, some confidence, or trust of those resources is self-empowering. I may experience grief over the loss of a significant person in my life. I may feel baffled at a problem I have engaged. I may leap for joy over an accomplished task. I know how to deal with these. I am in touch with my resources. Those resources may also be external, friends, colleagues, religious groups, counselors, law enforcement agents, etc. etc. etc. They are among the resources available to me to address my feelings, thoughts, and experiences. Being congruent in all this may not be a feel-good experience. I may feel awful. However, I know, or can find out, what I can use to help me deal with my life's situations whether I feel good about them or badly about them.

Rogers' (1961) concept of the Fully Functioning Person may be a good description of congruence. I also consider it a good description of self-actualizing. However, it probably is difficult to claim that the "Fully Functioning Person" is about congruence. I am though making that claim. I believe that the congruent person is fully functioning, in touch with the self and his/her experiences, thoughts, and feelings. I don't hold the Fully Functioning Person as some ideal superior person. What it means for me to be fully functioning is radically different than the person who is far more "intelligent" or "talented" than I am. The person who has experienced some sort of brain lesion may not be able to function at the same level that he or she did prior to the injury, but still may be able to fully function at the highest levels available within the context of the injury. I think there are some generalizations that can be applied no matter what "fully functioning" means to any given person.

I will present Rogers' characteristics of this state as best I can. He indicated the Fully Functioning Person is a process, a movement towards the "good life. I found that only scrambled the concept for me. So, I'm going to stick with phrase "Fully Functioning Person." Characteristics of this include: "an openness to experience" (p. 187); "increasingly existential living" (p. 188); "an increasing trust in his organism" (p. 189).

First, let me address openness to experience. This is personal. It is reflection on old stuff. I was shy, withdrawn, and kept to myself growing up. I was not aware of my impact on my peers. I shied away from events and activities with them. I could not even talk myself into playing football or baseball with my high school teams, even though I liked to play both games.

Thus, I did not share my feelings with anybody. I often felt sad and alone in the midst of a crowd, especially if they were having fun. When I did talk myself into playing football, the trips to away games were difficult experiences.

In this, there's not enough room to talk about dating and not dating. I didn't have a date until my senior year in high school. My attempts to get one were turned down, only adding to my reluctance to ask a girl out and probably contributing even more to my awkwardness in asking.

This experience of myself remained until I took clinical pastoral education via the Emory University Hospital system and found myself. By that, I mean I started to express myself. I was able to share pain, agony, anger, and with that able to share joy, celebration, and amazement.

I later did find out why I was shy. Being open to once experience sometimes means troubling others who in turn lash out with some variation of "who do you think you are" or "how dare you." People might take offense. Indeed, some do. Their reactions might be vicious with dismissiveness, anger, and manipulation. In relationship to that I found when I got negative responses, I felt guilty for having a negative impact on others. To this day, even though I feel I have reached a level of expressing myself, I also feel the discouragement, the pain, and the agony of people being disappointed in finding out what I believe, think, or experience. If I say, I am outraged, I discover that there are people who take offense at my outrage and become outraged. I then feel guilty for owning my feelings and telling others who respond in kind.

I can still slip into little bit of "poor me" in this. And I'm not very good at telling those people where to stick it, though I would like to. That does not mean that I won't do that. It means that there are occasions which, in the name of discretion, it is my experience to err on the side of empathy. And I will do so even if the person who is upset with me gives no indication that they even notice my being empathic. I have been able to function at a level of, feel the experience and do it anyway. That attitude has not given me Carte Blanche to do whatever I want when I want to. People can really be hurt. But it has given me courage, if courage is carrying on in the face of fear and/or guilt.

I'm making a brief case for being open to experience as not always being pleasant. It might be awful.

I also want to make a case for it being positive. That is joy and celebration and wonder are also easier to access. These tend to cancel out the negativity because there are more of those experiences. Still, one negative event can disrupt the positive.

The Fully Functioning Person is one who is in touch with those realities. It is not about suppression, denial, or the dreaded unconscious experience of repression. It is about the realities, good or bad, of the experiences of the Fully Functioning Person. It is about finding ways to get to the positive experiences while having negative experiences or setting aside the negative to experience the positive.

I am sure that virtually every person has experiences. Those experiences may be quite different in relationship to the myriad of situations in which we may find ourselves, but they are the person's experiences. One person may be afraid of a mouse. The other may look at that same mouse in the same setting and be awed.

Can I be open to my experiences? If so, I am congruent, and Fully Functioning.

Second, I will address "increasingly existential living." If the first point was difficult this perhaps more so.

I fancy myself as appreciating the concept of existentialism. I do not think I have a complex sophisticated grasp of that is in the terms of say Nietzsche or Tillich. Rather I think of it as dealing with the realities of life seen in the pain and suffering the agony of life as well as the wonders and marvels of living. I know that it is possible before I finish this work to have some catastrophe strike me or someone close to me. And if not, knowing that all I have to do is visit Facebook or read some news item about tragedy in the world. From the standpoint of a person of faith, the words of Jesus come to mind, "in the world you have tribulation, but take courage I have overcome the world., And tended to like the words "take courage" rather than the King James version which says, "be of good cheer." In fact, in the face of tension, and angst, I am not usually a good cheer. But I do believe one can take courage in the reality of adversity.

But the other part of that is positive, for I believe that being an existentialist, is also to be able to be aware of the beauty and the wonder of that which is around us: to enjoy the sight of a mama skunk carrying its young across a country road as it moves them to a new place; to look at a sunset on the Gulf of Mexico on the coast of Florida following evening thunderstorms and be blown away by the colors of orange and yellow and red as they mix together.

And thirdly, there is "an increasing trust in his organism." There is a movement towards and grasping the mind, body, and soul (spirit) work. Those vast resources mention previously enable persons to live quite well, even in during hardships. Not only can joy be trusted, but also sadness can be trusted. Further, one has a sense of significant control over how to engage life's experiences. I can find ways to overcome disappointment. I can find ways to experience happiness. I am human. I have trust in my abilities to deal with my personal resources.

Unconditional Positive Regard

I don't believe in "unconditional positive regard." I believe in deliberate positive regard. I cannot call my positive regard unconditional. I ask, if, in any given moment, acceptance does not exist, does that not make the acceptance conditional? If so, there are conditions surrounding the positive regard. Are there behaviors that the client might manifest that the therapist cannot accept? If you kill my goldfish, my positive regard is gone. As long as you don't harm me or those closest to me, I can maintain positive regard.

What I liked about the concept of unconditional positive regard when I first started struggling with it, was, I am in charge of my positive regard, not someone else. I still believe that to be true.

As I began to get involved in the person-centered community, I saw too much conflict, too much self-righteous indignation, too much judgmental ness. These showed up with condemnation that such and such behavior in the community was not person-centered. It showed up regarding new people who had room for embracing other theorists in their seeking to be person-centered, only to be brow beaten for not adhering to the real client-centered model.

David Cain (2010) did not affirm what I just wrote, but he did acknowledge the reality of differing slants regarding the approach. "At this point, one can no longer say that there is only one form of person-centered therapy . . . If one thing is certain, is that person-centered therapies will continue to evolve in future years as more is learned about how therapists and clients might engage more optimally with each other" (p. 43). These slants led to a host of conflicts about what is person-centered and thus violated in those conflicts the appearance of the adherents practicing what they preach. In conversations with various adherents, I keep hearing the conflict remains and at times is brutal.

I found that by abandoning the use of the word "unconditional" I didn't have to defend its use in the face of dissonant realities. I replaced it with one of the original concepts "acceptance." I now look at "acceptance" as the receiving the world of the other regardless of regard (positive, or negative). If I can do that, I have offered an important condition for growth and change. If I cannot, I have not offered such a condition.

Rogers (1989/1957) work introduced the concept of "unconditional positive regard" in 1957. I am using the material from 1989 which is a reprint. I am convinced that the label was consistent with his premises of acceptance, warmth, and positive regard. He acknowledged Standal as the contributor of the term, though I very seldom hear acknowledgment from the Person-centered community.

I didn't even know what Standal's first name is. I found it on Google Scholar, "Stanley."

Not believing in unconditional positive regard has made it difficult for me to present Rogers's position.

Rogers (1989/1957) definition of UPR was this:

> "To the extent that the therapist finds himself experiencing a warm acceptance of each aspect of the client's experience as being part of that client, is experiencing unconditional positive regard. This concept has been developed by Standal (8). It means that there are no *conditions* of acceptance, no feelings of 'I like you only *if* you are thus and so.' It means a 'prizing' of the person, as Dewey has used that term. It is at the opposite pole from a selective evaluating attitude – 'you are bad in these ways, good in those.' Involves as much feeling of acceptance for the client's expression of negative, 'bad,' painful, fearful, defensive, and normal feelings is for his expression of 'good,' positive, mature, confident, social feelings, as much acceptance of ways in which he is inconsistent as of ways in which he is consistent. It means a caring for the client, but not in a possessive way or in such a way as simply to satisfy this therapist's own needs. It means a caring for the client has a separate person, with permission to have his own feelings, his own experiences" (p. 225).

I cannot make a case for why Rogers calls this unconditional positive regard. Rogers (1942) stated, "the counselor accepts, recognizes, and clarifies these negative feelings . . . If the counselor is except these feelings he must be prepared to respond, not to the intellectual content of what the person is saying, but that the feeling which underlies it. Sometimes the feelings of deep ambivalences, sometimes their feelings of hostility. Sometimes their feelings of inadequacy. Whatever they are, counselor endeavors, they what he says and by what he does, to create an atmosphere in which the client can come to recognize that he has these negative feelings and can accept them as part of himself. . . ."(pp. 37).

This still holds true today whether one uses the term unconditional positive regard or acceptance. Thus, I still have no case for unconditional positive regard being a helpful word to augment or clarify "acceptance." Thorne (1992) wrote, "Rogers' concept of acceptance of which the term 'unconditional positive regard' is an elaboration, implies a caring by the therapist which is totally uncontaminated by judgments or evaluations of the thoughts, feelings or behaviour of the client. The therapist does not accept some aspects of the client and reject others. He or she experiences (and this cannot be simulated) and outgoing, positive, non-possessive warmth for the client. Such acceptance extends to the full range of the client's feelings and attitudes, from hostility and indifference to love and joy" (pp. 37).

In the 1989/1957 article, Rogers said in a footnote, "the phrase 'unconditional positive regard' may be an unfortunate one, since it sounds like an absolute, and all-or-nothing dispositional concept. It is probably evident from the description that completely unconditional positive regard would never exist except in theory. From a clinical and experiential point of view I believe the most accurate statement is that the effective therapist experiences unconditional positive regard for the client during many moments of his contact with him, yet from time to time he experiences only a conditional positive regard – and perhaps at times a negative regard, though this is not likely ineffective therapy. It is in this sense that unconditional positive regard exists as a matter of degree in any relationship" (p. 225).

I find nothing unconditional about unconditional positive regard and this statement only supports my position though a host of Person-Centered counselors, therapists, and theorists use it.

Empathic Understanding

Empathy to me is understanding. I don't get the reduplication. I don't know how one can enter the world of another as if, and not come away with verbal or nonverbal understanding.

I found the following material about a person named "Roger" which I believe captures something of the significance of empathy: (Nichols, 2009).

> "Roger's best friend in college was Derek. They were both political science majors and shared a passion for politics. Together they followed every detail of the Watergate investigation, relishing each new revelation as though they were a series of deliciously wicked Charles Addams cartoons. But as much as they took cynical delight in the exposure of corruption in the Nixon White House, their friendship went beyond politics. Roger remembered the wonderful feeling of talking to Derek for hours, impelled by the momentum of some deep and inexplicable sympathy. There was the pleasure of being able to say anything he wanted and the pleasure of hearing Derek say everything he'd always thought but never expressed. Unlike most of Roger's other friends, Derek wasn't a competitive conversationalist. He really listened. When they went to graduate schools in different cities, they kept up their friendship. Roger would visit Derek, or Derek would visit Roger, at least once a month. They'd play pool or see a movie and go out for Chinese food; and then afterward, no matter how late it got, they'd stay up talking. Then Derek got married, and things changed. Derek didn't become distant the way some friends do after

one marries, nor did Derek's wife dislike Roger. The distance that Roger felt was a small thing, but it made a big difference. "It's difficult to describe exactly, but I often end up feeling awkward and disappointed when I speak with Derek. He listens, but somehow he doesn't seem really interested anymore. He doesn't ask questions. He used to be involved rather than just accepting. It makes me sad. I still feel excited about the things going on in my life, but telling Derek just makes me feel unconnected and alone with them." Roger's lament says something important about listening. It isn't just not being interrupted that we want. Sometimes people appear to be listening but aren't really hearing. Some people are good at being silent when we talk. Sometimes they betray their lack of interest by glancing around and shifting their weight back and forth. At other times, however, listeners show no sign of inattention, but still we know they aren't really hearing what we have to say. It feels like they don't care" (Kindle Locations 228-246).

This brief description appears me to capture both understanding and non-understanding. It also has a flavor of acceptance in relationship to empathy. One might be hard pressed to say that empathy and acceptance can be separated. How does one really really really understand without acceptance?

I like the experience of empathy to two friends sitting on the front porch. They may talk about anything. They may complain about anything. They may celebrate a terrific event. They may engage in politics, religion, education or a host of topics. During the conversation, they might seem to shut out the world. That is, they may not seem to be anything else going on in the world. Suddenly, two hours goes by.

A long-standing definition of empathy if not the empathic process was presented (Rogers, 1951). "This formulation would state that it is the counselor's function to assume, in so far as he is able, the internal frame of reference of the client, to perceive the world as the client sees it, to perceive the client himself as he is seen by himself, to lay aside all perceptions from the external frame of reference while doing so, and to communicate something of this empathic understanding to the client" (p. 29). Rogers (1980) simply said of empathy "It means entering the private perceptual world of the other and becoming thoroughly at home in it" (p. 142). What is the person feeling, experiencing, thinking, and/or believing?

It is a front porch experience in therapy without the therapist sharing very much of his/her own feelings, experiences, thoughts, and beliefs. Instead, the focus is on the client, the other person.

Communication of Empathy and UPR

I am convinced that empathy and acceptance can be present, but the incongruent client may not be able to detect them. After all the client is in a state of mind whereby he/she has difficult accessing his or her own experiences. To be aware of the empathy and acceptance of the therapist may also be hard for the client to grasp.

I am also convinced that the presence of these factors remains necessary and sufficient even if the client doesn't consciously grasp their presence. Above, I may have essentially discarded psychological contact as necessary. Certainly, it is important. It though may be necessary for the client to continue in therapy. Without it, the client may not have grounds for continuing unless he/she sees progress. For in the presence of the necessary and sufficient conditions, the client is expressing him or herself and thus therapy is being offered and received.

Further, I believe the conditions are experienced at an unconscious level. I have some Process Theory presuppositions in this that experiences are "prehended" and thus influence other experiences (Jackson, 1981).

Rogers (1989/1957) wrote, "The final condition as stated is that the client perceives, to a minimal degree, the acceptance and empathy which the therapist experiences him. Unless some communication of these attitudes has been achieved, then such attitudes do not exist in the relationship as far as the client is concerned, and the therapeutic process could not, by our hypothesis, be initiated" (p. 226).

Maybe, maybe not.

Personally, though, I believe this brings us full circle back to the first condition, "psychological contact." I am asserting that the "psychological contact" increases the possibility of awareness regarding all the conditions, but particularly this last condition of perceiving the empathy and acceptance. I am not saying however, they are yoked and that one does not exist without the presence of another.

My Unknown Rogers

My unknown Rogers is about not meeting Carl Rogers. It is about not having person hubris that I know the Person-Centered Approach as virtually a walking encyclopedia of his ideas, and concepts. I tend not to believe the person who thinks he or she is correct about his/her understanding of Rogers. The unknown Rogers is also not about making some heretofore unknown information. I haven't found lost papers.

Instead, it is about sharing views as a person who has interacted with the approach for many years. If I am among those who appear to get Rogers while others don't, I have failed in communicating one perspective: that of only being able to share my views.

References

Cain, D. J. (2010). *Person-centered psychotherapies*. Washington, D.C.: American Psychological Association.

Jackson, G. E. (1981). *Pastoral care and process theology*. Washington, D.C.: University Press of America.

Jourard, S. M. (1971). *Self-disclosure: An experimental analysis of the transparent self*. New York: John Wiley & Sons.

Nichols, Michael P. (2009-02-16). *The Lost Art of Listening*, Second Edition: *How Learning to Listen Can Improve Relationships* (Kindle Locations 228-246). Guilford Publications. Kindle Edition.

Rogers, C. R. (1951). *Client-centered therapy: Its current practice, implications, and theory, with chapters*. Boston: Houghton Mifflin.

Rogers, C. (1961). *On becoming a person*. Boston: Houghton Mifflin.

Rogers, C. (1980). *A way of being*. Boston: Houghton Mifflin.

Rogers, C. R. (1986). Rogers, Kohut, and Erickson: A personal perspective on some similarities and differences. *Person-Centered Review*, 125-140.

Rogers, C. R. (1989/1957). The necessary and sufficient conditions of therapeutic personality change. In *The Carl Rogers reader*. (H. Kirschenbaum& V.L Henderson, Eds.(1989)). Boston: Houghton Mifflin.

Thorne, B., & Sanders, P. (2012). *Carl Rogers*. London: Sage.

Yalom, I. D. (1995). *The theory and practice of group psychotherapy*. New York: Basic Books.

Yalom, I. D. (2001). *The gift of therapy*. London: Piatkus.

The Unknown Tillich:

Glances from Far Away

If dealing with Rogers with whom I may have come within weeks of meeting personal were glances from afar, this is even more so for the unknown Tillich. Whatever I have to say about Tillich is from very far away. At least Rogers communicated in a way that I felt I could grasp. With Tillich, I feel like I step into the old 1960s television show, Rod Serling's "The Twilight Zone." Tillich is so abstract to me that I feel like I am attempting to deal with a foreign language.

Like Rogers, this material will not be about some newly founded works of Paul Tillich. I did not have any opportunity or near opportunity to meet Paul Tillich. "Glances from Far Away" are about failing to understand Tillich as well as never coming close to seeing him or meeting.

I have found dealing with giants cumbersome and intimidating. I could handle Rogers, but Tillich still leaves me scratching my head.

I have no clue what motivated San Diego to bring these two giants of differing fields together, but they did come together. Surely, their reputations were an important part of that joint event. I wonder if the theme might have been sort of what would happen when the secular meets the theological?

Yet, I am fascinated by Tillich. I suspect it is about Tillich's reputation, rather than the works I have attempted to explore. Tillich was a theologian that had to at least be acknowledged as I went through seminary. Ben Kline, at Columbia Theological Seminary, was recognized on campus as the Tillichian expert. I was impressed enough to take a course focusing on Tillich. I did not blow the top off the grading scale. I got a B, which for me at the time was pretty good.

Before I get too deep into this material, I hold Tillich as a closet Lutheran. If I am fortunate during the writing of this material, I will be able to show that. A chapter is dedicated to asserting that theme. If I pull it off, I will be successful. If not, I will remain scrambled. I don't mind dragging the reader into my bewilderment and lack of clarity. If I am lucky, the reader will join in saying "What?" If am even luckier the reader will say, I want to look at Tillich myself. Those that are experts on Tillich may be dismayed at my effort.

I have been dealing with a dialogue between Carl Rogers (with whom I believe I have some grasp) and Paul Tillich (about whom I believe I have appreciation, but feel I have little grasp). I can say that they do not speak the same language. Tillich's New Being and Ultimate Concern do not translate or equate well with Rogers' Self-Actualization, Congruence, or Fully Functioning Person. I'd like to make a case for their speaking the same language, but Tillich is a theologian who in the existential tradition is speaking theology. Rogers is psychologist who in the humanist tradition (a case might be made the existentialism is under that umbrella perhaps) who speaking in the arena of psychology. I have lived in both domains (theology and psychology), but my justification of that is hardly Tillichian, and I am finding it difficult to link to two arenas. I can theologize Rogers in my mind, but I cannot make Tillichian theology "Person-Centered" in my mind.

Recognizing my limits, I hope to share my take on a few of Paul Tillich's concepts. I will admit that doing so will be the Bowerization of those concepts. If one wants to know what Tillich said, I encourage people to read Tillich. I am capable only of sharing my perspectives. I have no guarantee they will accurately reflect Tillich.

Ultimate Concern

When I was exploring my interest in pastoral counseling there was standard phrase used regarding interactions that lacked clarity. "Can you unpack that?" It was simply an effort to get clarification.

No, I can't unpack "Ultimate Concern."

I really would like to find some "common ground" between the humanist Rogers, and the existential theologian, Tillich.

The best I can do is say that Rogers was raised in a conservative Calvinistic tradition, while Tillich was raised in a Lutheran tradition. Luther preceded Calvin, but it may be splitting hair to get the differences theologically. I would be satisfied to say both with strongly influenced by the Apostle Paul's writings. I also would say from my perspective that Luther was the one having to be courageous in terms of danger to his life, while, Calvin was the one who stirred the most controversy. I hardly ever hear concerns from colleagues about being a Lutheran, but many a battle has occurred about be a Calvinist. "A few indeed I have seen draw back to perdition, chiefly through a fear of being 'righteous overmuch.' And here and there one has fallen into Calvinism, or turned to the Moravians" (Wesley, 1746, pp. 236-237). Myself, I have tended to like both Luther and Calvin, but fancy myself being more familiar with Calvin, though often overwhelmed by his wordiness.

From here, whatever I have to say about Tillich's position reflect only my grasp in relationship to presuppositions about Tillich being a Lutheran, not a Calvinist. I dare not claim to speak for Tillich, except when I do. I do have a little audacity, after all I am offering this chapter not having a clue what I am writing about, save I can share my views.

Tillich (2001) opens chapter 1 saying, "Faith is the state of being ultimately concerned: the dynamics of faith are the dynamics of man's ultimate concern. Man, like every living being, is concerned about many things, above all about those which condition his very existence, such as food and shelter. But man, in contrast to other living beings, has spiritual concerns—cognitive, aesthetic, social, political. Some of them are urgent, often extremely urgent, and each of them as well as the vital concerns can claim ultimacy for a human life or the life of a social group. (p. 1)

I wrote above that I would like to find common ground between Tillich and Rogers. In a feeling of futility, my best link here regarding Rogers and Tillich would be to say this might be a way to speak to the "fully functioning person (Rogers, 1961). That person could indeed have characteristics of being cognitive, aesthetic, social, and political. The fully functioning person would likely be a person "concerned about many things." In my bias, I believe the following statement reflects yet another slant of similarity here: "Faith as ultimate concern is an act of the total personality. It happens in the center of the personal life and includes all its elements. Faith is the most centered act of the human mind" (p. 4). Tillich (2001) essentially repeats that later: "Faith is a total and centered act of the personal self, the act of unconditional, infinite and ultimate concern" (pp. 9-10).

I also find myself wondering if Tillich's statement is all that far from the definition of faith found in Hebrews 11:1 (KJV): "Now faith is the substance of things hoped for, the evidence of things not seen."

It does not appear to me that Tillich limits this stance to what might be consider positive by some. Thus, blind nationalism, even Satan worship, may fit into Tillich's concept. It has nothing to do with what the concern is about. It has everything to do with having an "ultimate concern." Tillich (2001) did assert in the context of the Judeo-Christian tradition, "An example—and more than an example—is the faith manifest in the religion of the Old Testament. It also has the character of ultimate concern in demand, threat and promise. The content of this concern is not the nation—although Jewish nationalism has sometimes tried to distort it into that—but the content is the God of justice, who, because he represents justice for everybody and every nation, is called the universal God, the God of the universe. He is the ultimate concern of every pious Jew, and therefore in his name the great commandment is given: 'You shall love the Lord your God with all your heart, and with all your soul, and with all your might' (Deut. 6:5)" (pp. 2-3).

For adherents of the person-centered approach one aspect, if not a significant one, is a commitment to the Rogers (1957) necessary and sufficient conditions. Assuming I have a bit of a grasp of this concept, this commitment is an ultimate concern within the Person-Centered Approach.

With Tillich, this "ultimate concern" which he calls faith is a kind of specialized ultimate concern. "Where there is faith there is an awareness of holiness . . . The awareness of the holy is awareness of the presence of the divine, namely of the content of our ultimate concern." (p. 14).

Faith for Tillich carries courage. But courage for what? Essentially, courage to engage existential anxiety. This aspect of anxiety has long been part of my awareness of what Tillich is about as an existentialist. Without a formal definition, I have asserted that existentialism is about dealing with the realities of life, in particular, its harsh realities and especially finiteness. "The description of anxiety as the awareness of one's finitude is sometimes criticized as untrue from the point of view of the ordinary state of the mind. Anxiety, one says, appears under special conditions but is not an ever-present implication of man's finitude. Certainly, anxiety as an acute experience appears under definite conditions. But the underlying structure of finite life is the universal condition which makes the appearance of anxiety under special conditions possible.

In the same way doubt is not a permanent experience within the act of faith. But it is always present as an element in the structure of faith" (Tillich, 2001, p. 24).

Personally, I have connected this existential anxiety with Tillich and estrangement. "It must be acknowledged that man is in a state of estrangement from his true nature. Thus, the use of his reason and the character of his faith are not what they essentially are and, therefore, ought to be. This leads to actual conflicts between a distorted use of reason and an idolatrous faith" (p. 89). Out of touch with himself, the human being has no basis for being grounded himself. There is no, or at least a weak, foundation for the grounding.

Carl Rogers (1957) mentions in his "Necessary and Sufficient Conditions" that the client comes for counseling as one who is incongruent, and thus anxious. It is here that the theological, the philosophical, and psychological have common ground. There might be in this hope of psychotherapy, in particular, that of the person-centered approach, in which congruence of the person is more fully realized. The person becomes more fully the person he or she truly is. Thus, the anxiety would decrease. The secular person though is limited to the secular completion or fulfillment. The faith person is united to a person beyond the secular limits, being the creature that God had intended with a greater awareness of God. The position of decreasing anxiety though for Tillich seems to be related to the chronic anxiety of estrangement. This can be suppressed I suppose by distraction in everyday activities, but estrangement is always lurking even in "faith" of the traditional Christian stance.

Estrangement

While Carl Rogers wrote about incongruence (which won't be visited here), Paul Tillich addressed estrangement. This is philosophical and theological issue impacting the personal (psychological). Tillich though is a theologian. Thus, his comments are theological, not psychological. "But revelation is revelation to man in his state of corrupted faith and corrupted rationality. And the corruption, although broken in its final power, is conquered but not removed" (Tillich, 2001, p. 91). The estranged self, being, or person, (whatever one's preference on this), is corrupted. That his broken. "The symbol of the 'fall of Adam' implies a concept of man's essential nature, of his conflict with himself, of his estrangement from himself" (p. 109). While I indicated that I would not explore Roger's position, the stance for Tillich is not all that far from Rogers.

For Rogers incongruence is not a permanent issue. For Tillich estrangement is, sort of. That the corruption constantly lurks. "Only God can reunite the estranged with himself" (p. 134). It is only overcome to a degree via ultimate concern. "Out of this double corruption there arise new conflicts between faith and reason and with them the quest for a new and superior revelation. The history of faith is a permanent fight with the corruption of faith, and the conflict with reason is one of its most conspicuous symptoms. The decisive battles in this fight are the great revelatory events, and the victorious battle would be a final revelation in which the distortion of faith and reason is definitely overcome" (p. 91).

"The concern of faith is identical with the desire of love: reunion with that to which one belongs and from which one is estranged" (p. 130). The interest of psychotherapy is to grasp the self that one truly is (Bower, 2003).

The scientific and the faith models are different paradigms. Their jargons reflect different perspectives of looking at reality. "Modern psychology is afraid of the concept of soul because it seems to establish a reality which is unapproachable by scientific methods and may interfere with their results. This fear is not unfounded; psychology should not accept any concept which is not produced by its own scientific work. Its function is to describe man's processes as adequately as possible, and to be open to replacement of these descriptions at any time" (pp. 95-96).

Personally, I move back and forth between the two disciplines and my bias finds similarities. Yet, I am hard pressed to make sense of that for others. Science has influenced my creationism in regard to faith and origins of the universe. Faith has allowed me to be awed by concepts of infinity, at least within the limits of my finite grasp of infinite.

So too, I am equally amazed at estrangement in relationship to my concept of sin being estrangement that reflects corruption and distortion of every aspect of being. Science often shows me brokenness.

Tillich's concept of estrangement seems to me too important to me in relationship to the human being to the ultimate concern, or faith, or God. It helps me have a concept of why it is do difficult to have a traditional Christian faith, and why there is so much brokenness.

Rogers' concept of congruence does not allow one to go past being out of touch with the self, the experiences, and feelings of the person. It can in essence be fixed by a person getting in touch with his or her personal resources. There is always the possibility that creating an environment rich in the conditions of empathy, acceptance, and genuineness will facilitate movement that includes the possibility of being the "fully functioning" person one truly is.

Tillich's concept of faith allows estrangement to be overcome via ultimate concern, but still allows for brokenness to remain at the same time. Yet his concepts or those of any person of faith cannot be depended upon to be final. And science cannot be either. "The truth of faith cannot be confirmed by latest physical or biological or psychological discoveries—as it cannot be denied by them" (p. 98).

New Being

There is no "new being" without "being." There is no need to speak of a "new being" if there wasn't something about the "being" that needs to be "new." Thus, the concept of "estrangement" is significant to capture the need for "new." There is no functioning as a "being" without "courage." Courage is the affirmation of one's essential nature, one's inner aim or entelechy, but it is an affirmation which has in itself the character of 'in spite of'" (Tillich, 1980, p. 4). Courage then is about ultimate concern which enable the affirmation of one's essential nature. Movement towards overcoming estrangement then would need courage. As pointed out above, Tillich asserts this can only take place with God. For Rogers, a psychotherapist can help with this facilitating the client's discovery to the self one truly is (Bower, 2003) and God is not needed.

We are dealing with theology and not psychology. The courage here is not about congruence and incongruence, it is about the finite, limited, anxious being who must deal with threats to his or her non-being. This is not the person who is disarray with his or her innate self. This the person alone in a vast universe who must deal with and face being a finite creature. The reality that one may fall out of existence and indeed some assert that returns to non-being is the reality. "The courage to be is the courage to affirm one's own reasonable nature over against what is accidental in us" (Tillich, 1980, p. 13).

I am not going to struggle with what is meant by "courage." I probably shouldn't try to tackle "new being" either. However, that is precisely what I am going to do. I am going to try to share how the concept of "new being" impacts me and share what I can of that impact.

In Tillich, I sense two aspects of the "new being." The first aspect is a being, one that transcends, the old being. One who is not actually synonymous with the original being, but different. I have room to say that the "new being" is the Christ dressed up in contemporary jargon. The Christ is too foreign for the contemporary human being. The second aspect, is the overcoming of the estranged nature with the estranged person becoming "new." Estrangement is dealt with and the person becomes in sync with him or herself.

It appears to me in Tillich (1980), that being is not about existence, that is about biochemistry, physiological, or whatever makes up a being, a person in this case. This physical aspect is rather the result of a process or "becoming." In this sense, it may be similar to what Carl Rogers consistently wrote about "the actualizing tendency," or "self-actualization." Tillich contrasts this with "nonbeing." Personally, that is harder to get at than "being." At least "being" has some sort of experience surrounding it, with words attached. "Nonbeing" does not. For an infinite number of years before any of us entered into our personal process of being and becoming, there was "nonbeing." We have no words for that. Perhaps that is why there is so much anxiety. We like, at least it appears most of us do, our "being" and process of becoming.

If Tillich is correct, "Nonbeing is one of the most difficult and most discussed concepts" (1980, p. 32), there is futility in discussing it in that considering we have no words to describe it. We didn't even know we didn't exist. Allegedly, some of anxiety in life is about the return to that state. "Cowards die many times before their deaths; The valiant never taste of death but once. Of all the wonders that I yet have heard, It seems to me most strange that men should fear; Seeing that death, a necessary end, Will come when it will come" William Shakespeare (1564-1616), Julius Caesar. Act ii, Sc. 2. It may also be correct to say, that it also may be true that "nonbeing" is the most avoided of concepts. "Anxiety is the state in which a being is aware of its possible nonbeing" (Tillich, 1980, p. 35).

I am writing in a state of being. I am not writing in a state of nonbeing. That could change quickly, or my process of being may remain for many more short years.

As far as I am concerned this is where Rogers and Tillich part company as Rogers is dealing with congruent and incongruent aspects of "being." His approach is about psychology, psychotherapy, and its cousins, not theology.

Tillich is also ontological and thus not just theological. He is thus philosophical as well. That is not to say, Rogers isn't philosophical. That is to say, Rogers is about helping, while Tillich is about reflecting on the intellectual side of "being." Tillich does it speaking of Spinoza, Nietzsche, Hegel, Kant, Heidegger, Sartre, Whitehead and others. Rogers dealt with Goldberg and hints of others in the philosophical realm. Rogers it seems to be was indebted to the Renaissance. He had a powerful belief in the resourcefulness of humankind.

But I am finding the concept of "nonbeing" distracting. I am trying to grasp what Tillich is addressing in his concept of "being." Yet, can one speak of "being" without speaking of "nonbeing" or at least the awareness. I find myself wondering if the concept of "new being" might essentially be about the ultimate overcoming of "nonbeing."

Here I feel it appropriate to leave myself and the reader hanging with not further development. This is part of the angst not having solutions to "nonbeing." However, part of "new being" is its indescribable possibilities and potentials. Perhaps in that Tillich may have had a sense of eternity, after all his roots were in the Christian tradition.

References

Bower, D. (2003). *Person-centered/client-centered: Discovering the self that one truly is.* Lincoln, NE: iUniverse.

Rogers, C. R. (1957). The necessary and sufficient conditions of therapeutic personality change. *Journal of Consulting Psychology,* 1957, Vol 21, 95–203.

Rogers, C. (1961). *On becoming a person.* Boston: Houghton Mifflin.

Tillich, P. (1980). *The courage to be* (The Terry Lectures Series). New Haven, CN: Yale University Press. Kindle Edition.

Tillich, P. (2001). *Dynamics of faith.* New York, NY: (Perennial Classics), HarperCollins.

Wesley, J. (1746). The principles of a Methodist farther explained. In Rubert E. Davies Ed., 1989, *The works of John Wesley: Vol. 9, The Methodist societies: history, nature, and design* (pp.159-237). Nashville, TN: Abingdon Press.

Finale:

A Brief Closing

I tackled this project with delusions of grandeur. I mere mortal diving into a historic interaction. I make not claim that these two giants in their fields getting together caused any particular stir in either of their fields. I don't even know how many people were present to hear them when they met.

As part of the project, I had hoped to claim a chapter on Rogers' as a closet Calvinist and argue in it that Rogers essential remythologized Calvinism. However, when I looked at the material, I kept thinking, what makes Calvin Calvinist? What is unique about his stance that such a brand emerged. What of that would Rogers have secularized that would be different from say Wesley's position. I simply found attempting to highlight the uniqueness was presumptuous on my part.

Also, I wanted to claim that Tillich was a closet Lutheran. Hereto, I wanted to say Tillich remythologized Luther. I have felt when I read Tillich, I saw Luther. However, again I said there is such an overlap in the stances, Luther, Calvin, Wesley, and a host of others in Protestant domain that I would have trouble saying that Tillich was a closet Lutheran.

I might be tempted to say that Rogers and Tillich were closet Christians, save for Rogers took a secular path and Tillich is regarded as a Christian theologian. Tillich then wouldn't be a closet Christian.

So, I'll leave all this alone, frustrated perhaps with my clutter on these issues and thus feeling unfinished.

Printed in the United States
By Bookmasters